If you thought vegan food was brown and bland, think again.

V is for Vegan is the cookbook that blows that myth out of the water. Kerstin Rodgers' 150 recipes are game-changing, with easy ideas for flavor bombs like homemade vegan parmesan and pesto, breakfast treats, stunning soups and salads, dips, snacks, condiments, and spice mixes, naturally vegan dinners, and desserts you never thought possible without eggs or dairy.

This is the essential book for anyone who's ever thought about cutting down their meat or dairy intake, who's already vegan or vegetarian and wants to cook imaginative dishes, and for people who simply love great-tasting food. Creative, unique and packed with tips and advice, *V is for Vegan* will change the way you think about vegan cooking.

V
is for
vegan

KERSTIN RODGERS

Photography by Jan Baldwin

QUADRILLE

Unusual Ingredients

Contents

Introduction

What Do Vegans Eat?

This is the question most people ask. It is a plant-based diet.

In other words, if no animals were used in the ingredients of the dish, it's vegan.

Is It Easy?

The truth is that a vegan or vegetarian cook works harder.

There is more prep with vegetables than any other foodstuff. Think of the scrubbing, peeling, chopping, and blanching.

Although there are quick, simple dishes in this book, for the intrepid cook who wants to stretch their capabilities and expand their repertoire, there are also more complicated recipes.

The vegan cook must also work on flavor. There is no instant umami (savory) flavor coming from the Maillard (browning) reactions of seared flesh. But you can accomplish these flavor boosts in vegan cooking too. The vegan cook also draws on food from around the world to provide variety. The vegan cook is adventurous with ingredients.

Simple Food, Simply Cooked?

While I'm a great believer in simplicity, letting the ingredient take center stage, some vegans use complex cooking techniques to prepare their dishes. With the effort it takes to become vegan, most vegans spend time preparing their meals. This means that they will research and discover cutting-edge food preparation and rediscover old forgotten techniques.

Substitutes

Vegans use substitutes to replace animal products. In this book you will find recipes to make your own vegan substitutes for milk, butter, cheese, yogurt, and mayonnaise. As a cook I don't go for mock meats such as TVP (Textured Vegetable Protein) or "facon" (fake bacon). I prefer to use natural, unprocessed foods.

What Vegans Don't Eat & Why

"The greatness of a nation and its moral progress can be judged by the way its animals are treated." Mahatma Gandhi

Vegans have two primary objections to eating animal-derived food: ethical and environmental. For the former, some people simply feel uncomfortable eating sentient food and have strong feelings about animal welfare. For the latter, industrial livestock farming is undeniably having a disastrous effect on the environment. Most modern farming is industrial. Only a tiny proportion of animals are reared on a traditional farm.

So even if you don't become a full-time vegan, lowering your industrial meat and farmed fish intake is good for you, good for the planet, and good for animals. The only direct power we have is as consumers, so unless you know the source of your animal product, don't buy it.

Here is some information if you are thinking of going vegan for ethical reasons. No dogma, no guilt trip; just some information to think about.

Meat

We never used to eat this much flesh: meat eating has gone up by 300% over the last 50 years. Yet the price of meat and fish as a proportion of our income has plummeted. This can only be achieved by treating industrially farmed animals very badly.

Cattle need water, feed, and land. Our beef addiction destroys rainforests. As Dr. Mark Post, scientist and creator of synthetic lab meat, comments, "It takes 3½ oz [100 g] of plant food to create ½ oz [15 g] of meat; this isn't an efficient use of our resources."

Not only do industrially farmed livestock have terrible lives, it affects our environment. One instance: pig manure from industrial farming is on such a scale that it is leaking into the water table. People that live near these factory farms have asthma and other health problems.

Over the last few decades, there have been endless scandals regarding the cheap meat available in our stores, from Mad Cow Disease to the horse meat scandal. Meat eaters have no idea what they are eating.

Dairy

Consuming dairy, you might think, does not harm animals. But the dairy industry, under the system of intensive factory farming, is cruel. Cows left to their own devices live, on average, to be 20 years old, but industrial dairy cows live a mere 4 or 5 years. Cows are kept constantly pregnant and lactating, and given hormones to grow to adolescence more quickly. The milking machines cause pain and injury. The tiny baby bulls are removed from their mothers within one day of being born and are kept in the dark,

then killed as veal, while the calves are removed at one day old and fed milk replacers. Baby cows don't get the milk; we do. But that milk often contains pesticides, pus, hormones, and antibiotics.

Eggs

Only female chickens produce eggs, so in industrial egg production the males are disposed of, often while still alive. All industrial egg production, even if "free-range" or cage-free," is cruel. The hens are kept in crowded conditions, their beaks are amputated, they are pushed to produce more eggs than is natural, which deprives their bodies of calcium, and as soon as their egg production goes down, they are killed.

Fish

Problems include over-fishing, to the point that many species (cod, tuna) will be extinct within 50 years. Farmed fish eat their own body weight in antibiotics to combat disease from overcrowding. Dredge-net fishing, using nets the size of several football fields, is a crude commercial way of fishing, killing dolphins and sea turtles (by-catch) along with the fish. Radiation is also a problem, due to the Fukushima nuclear disaster.

Jelly

Jelly and gelatin are made from cows' hooves. Vegan, plant-based alternatives (carrageen, agar-agar) are available, but so far do not have all the qualities of jelly, which melts at body temperature.

Honey

Most honey comes from farmed bees, and just like other industrially farmed creatures, they are mistreated. Their hives are artificially fed with sugar or corn syrup rather than nectar, so their honey is of poor quality. Bee numbers are declining because of pesticides, antibiotics, being restricted to the nectar of monoculture crops, and mobile phones messing with their navigation systems. If you buy honey, find out about natural beekeeping, which respects the hive.

Finally, each bee produces about a teaspoon of honey during its lifetime. Bees produce honey because they need it, to survive winter.

Alcohol?

There are vegan wines, beer, or "natural" wines. But wine doesn't have animal products in it, I hear you say. Actually, egg whites, fish bladders, albumen, milk protein, and shellfish are used for clarification. Most "natural" wines (which contain no additives or sulfur) are vegan. Most hard alcohol is vegan.

Vegan Cosmetics & Clothes

Dedicated vegans use vegan-friendly cosmetics, nail polish, shampoo, and conditioner. Pearlized eyeshadow is created from oyster shells.

Some vegans will also avoid medicines that contain animal products; however, all medicines are currently tested on animals prior to being used by humans.

Strict vegans do not wear leather, fur, wool, ivory, or bone jewelry, silk (made from silkworms boiled alive), feathers, or pearls. Pearls used to be very rare, but nowadays are farmed industrially.

Brief History of Veganism

Veganism is not a newfangled thing. In Ancient Greece, philosophers such as Pythagoras argued that both humans and animals should be treated with respect. By the late 4th century BC, a debate had developed between two opposing schools of thought: while Theophrastus suggested that animals possess reason, Aristotle disagreed.

Around the time of Jesus Christ, many sects discussed the mistreatment of other species. There is a long tradition of people refusing to eat animal-derived foods based on either religion or philosophy. Many devout Christians

assert that Jesus was a vegetarian, and cite the commandment "Thou shalt not kill" and the Book of Daniel.

Centuries later, in the UK, anti-monarchist Oliver Cromwell passed animal welfare laws (1653) and Puritanism became associated with animal protection.

During the French enlightenment, humanist philosopher Rousseau argued in *A Discourse on Inequality* (1755) that animals are sentient beings. Later he encouraged a vegetarian diet for children.

During the early 19th century in Britain, moral discourse advocated restraint with regard to eating meat, and there was a parallel between better treatment of animals and the anti-slavery movement.

Dr. William Lambe wrote the first ever vegan diet book *Water and Vegetable Diet in Consumption, Scrofula, Cancer, Asthma, and Other Chronic Diseases* (1815). The early 19th century was also the romantic period, which valued compassion and nature, and poet Percy Bysshe Shelley, his wife Mary, plus their friend Byron all became vegan for periods of time. Shelley lived for a while in a vegan commune in Bracknell. He wrote *A Vindication of Natural Diet* (1813), while Mary Shelley wrote the celebrated book *Frankenstein* (1818) whose famous "monster" is vegan! At the same time, more fruits and vegetables were available in Europe, making a meat-free diet more accessible.

In 1824 in the UK, the RSPCA was formed by anti-slavery parliamentarian William Wilberforce and others, including Lewis Gompertz who published *Moral Inquiries on the Situation of Man and of Brutes*. Gompertz was possibly the first "freegan"—he thought that if the animal died of natural causes, it was fine to eat meat, and if a calf died naturally, it was fine to drink the milk of the mother.

In the USA, there was a similar drive toward a plant-based diet in the early to mid-19th century, for health and spiritual reasons.

Influential author, philosopher, and abolitionist Henry David Thoreau ate only plant-based foods. Dr. Sylvester Graham, creator of Graham (whole-wheat) flour, published *Lectures on the Science of Human Life* (1839), advocating a diet of plant food and water. Bronson Alcott, father of Louisa May Alcott who wrote *Little Women*, was an advocate of the "vegetable diet." He opened a vegan commune in New England called Fruitlands. Alcott was also an abolitionist who argued for women's rights. Alcott then traveled to England where the first vegetarian school, Alcott House School, was opened just outside of London.

Back in the UK, William Horsell created the London Vegetarian Association (1847), and then published *Hydropathy for the People: with Plain Observations on Drugs, Diet, Water, Air, and Exercise*. Horsell's wife, Elizabeth, was also an active vegetarian and writer. When Horsell died, she went on to open a vegetarian girl's boarding school.

Three years later, The American Vegetarian Society was formed, led by Sylvester Graham and Russell Thacher Trall; the latter, a naturopathic doctor, published the first official "vegan" cookbook (1854).

In Germany, Gustav Schlickeysen published *Fruit and Bread—A Scientific Diet* (1875), which is vegan, fruitarian, and raw-foodarian.

1886: Henry Salt, master at Eton, published *A Plea for Vegetarianism* and coined the phrase "animal rights." (UK)

1887: Dr. Kellogg, inventor of the cornflake, was also vegan. He was a great promoter of soy products and rediscovered soy milk, used for centuries in Chinese cuisine, as part of a healthy, plant-based diet. (USA)

1900: Maximilian Bircher-Benner invented Bircher muesli. He was strongly influenced by the writings of Schlickeysen. (Switzerland)

1910: The publication of the first British vegan cookbook *No Animal Food and Nutrition, and Diet with Vegetable Recipes* by Rupert Wheldon.

1931: Mahatma Gandhi spoke at the London Vegetarian Society. Ghandi was influenced by the works of Thoreau and Salt.

1944: The invention of the word "vegan": Donald Watson, a Yorkshireman, coined the term and founded the Vegan Society. Watson lived a long, healthy life, dying in 2005 at the age of 95.

Vegan Religions

Rastas
Buddhists
Some Hindus including:
Hare Krishna
Brahma Kumaris
Jain

Know Your "egans" and Your "arians"

Vegans: eat no animal products whatsoever.

Pescatarians: will not eat meat, red or white, but will eat fish.

Pollotarians: will not eat meat from a mammal, but will eat chicken.

Freegans: a portmanteau word combining "free" and "vegan;" freegans do not buy animal products. This is an anti-consumerist, anti-food waste movement, so they will eat animal products if they would otherwise be discarded.

Flexitarians: are semi-vegetarian. They occasionally eat meat. These are people who are "meat reducers", that is, trying to reduce the amount of meat they eat, or at the very least, trying to source meat from ethical suppliers. They are probably the biggest sector.

Vegetarians

Ovo-lacto-vegetarians: will eat plant foods, plus eggs and dairy.

Lacto-vegetarians: will eat dairy, but no eggs.

Ayurvedics: are vegan, but do not eat garlic, mushrooms, or onions because these are supposed to "excite" the body.

Raw foodists: only eat raw, uncooked food (cooked at less than 115°F [46°C]), as cooked food loses many nutritional benefits. They often use sprouted or fermented foods. They sometimes eat raw fish, eggs, and meat.

Fruitarians: only eat fruit, berries, seeds, and nuts.

Juicearians: exist on consuming only smoothies and juices made from fruit and vegetables.

Breatharians: don't eat food, they only need sunlight and fresh air. Don't try this at home.

Knowledge is Power

A vegan diet is easier
than you think. Basically,
you can eat anything that
is derived from plants,
and it's amazing when you
discover what flavors can be
achieved without meat. This
chapter will shed some light
on the hordes of amazing
ingredients and foodstuffs
you can stock up on, or make
yourself. Armed with this
knowledge, you can be bold
in the kitchen. And you'll
never run out of ideas for
how to pep up your dinner.

Umami Flavor Bombs: The Vegan Toolkit

Here is a toolbox of "flavor bombs" that will instantly pep up your food.

Umami Boosters

Anything preserved or fermented increases the umami (savoriness) factor in food. Some of these ingredients you will know; others may be new to you. The money you save on cutting out animal products can be put toward some of these interesting ingredients.

Mushrooms are very umami: apart from the standard ones such as button or brown, splash out from time to time on shiitake, chanterelles, or morels (the latter are very expensive even in season, but they are gorgeous little cylindrical sponges of flavor). Dried mushrooms such as porcini can, when rehydrated, boost savoriness very effectively.

Huitlacoche is a Mexican fungus that grows on corn. Buy it canned from Mexican online stockists and use a mere smear to add intense flavor.

Truffles are the most luxurious fungus you can buy. A few shavings of this on pasta or in a creamy cashew cheese gratin can transform the dish. Who says veganism isn't high class?

Marmite is a favorite ingredient of mine. Use it to flavor stews, soups, and pasta, or on toast.

The best quality soy sauce tends to be Japanese, and rather more expensive than Chinese. Shoyu is the Japanese name for soy sauce. Within Chinese cooking there are light and dark soy sauces; dark soy sauce contains caramel and is used for cooking, to deepen color, while light soy is added to cooked food for enhancing flavor, almost like salt. Tamari (Japanese for "puddle") is gluten-free: unlike soy sauce, it doesn't use wheat; rather, it is the liquid content of soybean miso. Alternative soy-like sauces include Maggi Liquid Seasoning (which contains the herb lovage) and Bragg Liquid Aminos. Both are delicious.

Nutritional yeast flakes are used by everyone in the vegan world and are the secret ingredient of many recipes—a good replacement for cheesy flavor. It's amazing how a few yeast flakes can transform the flavor of a dish.

Vegan "Parmesan"

Makes a handful

3 Tbsp nutritional yeast

½ cup [50 g] pecans

Pinch of sea salt

In a food processor, grind the ingredients to a coarse, crumbly powder. Add to pasta, potatoes, polenta etc.

Miso is a fermented grain paste and one of the oldest foods in Japan. It comes in light and dark forms, is red, white, or brown, and can be made from barley, rice, buckwheat, rye, or millet. You can buy it from Japanese stores or online. Stir it into soups, spread it over broiled vegetables, whisk it into salad dressings, or use as a dip.

You may be surprised to know that chocolate is fermented. Do like the Mexicans and use it in savory as well as sweet foods—for instance the mole on page 142.

Tomato paste is an intense umami ingredient, good for soups and pasta sauce and as a base sauce for pizza. You can make your own—a good idea if you come by a large amount of cheap tomatoes in season. Peel and seed them, add 1 tsp salt for every 6 tomatoes, and cook them on a low simmer in a heavy pot in the oven for several hours. Tomatoes are one of the few foods that have more minerals and vitamins after cooking than raw.

Liquid smoke is a cheaty way to get a smoky flavor in your food. It's particularly gorgeous with beans or tofu and it's available in many supermarkets.

Citrus

There is so much more to the world of citrus than oranges and lemons, although I do like to use the zest of these well-known fruits as a last-minute reviver on many of my dishes. Zested lemon is reported to be good for its antiseptic qualities and to deter fatigue. By the way, it's the white pith that is bitter, not the yellow skin.

My latest citrus crush is **Bengali lime**, a large knobbly green fruit with floral notes which I discovered in a local Bangladeshi grocery store. Do check ethnic stores if you live in a city. I've also made preserved lemons from tiny Indian yellow limes, found hanging mysteriously in a brightly colored plastic net at the store around the corner from me.

Japanese yuzu has come to the fore in the last few years. Although it's difficult at present to get fresh

yuzu in the US, you can buy the juice, the paste, and ponzu, a yuzu/soy sauce. In the States there are Meyer lemons, also very floral. If you ever come across a kaffir lime, or indeed the plant, buy it. Not only will you have fresh kaffir lime for your Thai curries, but also use of the leaves.

I've also used **kumquats**, small oval orange fruit with a sweet skin.

Grapefruit farmers are growing new, sweeter cultivars, but bitter foods are good for you. too.

Pomelo is an Asian fruit, not unlike grapefruit, which I've used in the oriental-influenced salad on page 99.

Preserved Lemons, Satsumas, & Limes

(Photo on page 10.)

Makes 1½ cups [350 ml]

8 to 10 small Indian lemons (or 5 to 6 big lemons), limes, or satsumas

8¾ oz [250 g] rock salt

Juice of 5 lemons

Sterilize a 1½-cup [360-ml] jar by washing it thoroughly in hot soapy water, rinsing well, and then placing it in an oven preheated to 325°F [160°C] for 15 minutes. Sterilize the lid in boiling water for 15 minutes, with the rubber seal if the jar has one.

Meanwhile, wash the outside of all the citrus, and cut into quarters, without cutting all the way through, so that the 4 sections are attached at one end. Pack the salt inside the fruit, leaving the filled citrus in a bowl until the jar is ready.

Put a ¼-in [6-mm] layer of salt in the bottom of the hot, sterilized jar, then carefully fill with the salt-stuffed citrus, sprinkling a little salt between the layers. Press down once you have filled the jar, and top up with the lemon juice, and some water if necessary, to cover the fruit. Close the jar and keep an eye on it for the next 3 or 4 days, ensuring that the level of liquid does not dip below the fruit. Once you are confident that the fruit will remain submerged, store for 6 weeks in a cool, dark place before using it, finely sliced and added to grain dishes.

Useful Spices

I mention these spices, as you may not be aware of just how fab they are. Do regularly inspect and chuck spices—out-of-date ones are worse than useless, tasting like old moths. Keep them in a cool, dark place.

Achiote is like the Mexican version of saffron and hard to describe! Apart from adding a deep rusty color, it also imparts a kind of savory muddy clay flavor. It's good, I promise.

Saffron is one of the most expensive spices in the world, made from crocus stamens. A mere pinch adds new depth to any dish. I make saffron and tomato spaghetti sauce, lifting this classic, well-known dish above the ordinary (see page 126).

Ras el hanout is Arabic for something approximating "the best of the shop." Every family has its own version, but it's a ground mixture of spice and rose petals. It can be bought at most supermarkets nowadays, so add it to dips and North African/Arabic dishes.

Sumac is a citrusy berry, very popular in Middle Eastern cookery. It is now widely available. Sprinkle ground sumac over roast vegetables, pumpkin, squash, and dips.

Chinese five-spice contains Sichuan pepper, cloves, cinnamon, fennel seeds, and star anise, and is good in stir-fries and on tofu.

Japanese seven-spice or **shichimi** is a blend of chili, orange peel, black and white sesame seeds, hemp seeds, ground ginger, nori, and sansho.

Black limes are dried limes often used in Persian cooking. Crumble them into bean dishes or rice to add a sour flavor.

Sweet smoked paprika, especially the Spanish kind called pimentón de la Vera, instantly gives depth to any dish—some say it even tastes a bit like bacon. Hungarian paprika, however, retains its red color during cooking.

Pickled & Preserved Flavor Intensifiers

I love sweet and salty together, and most pickles require acidity too, to create an "agrodolce" zing to your food. Olives, capers, pickled peppercorns, and preserved plums can be bought in jars to augment and counterpoint. Chutneys and atchars perform the same function, adding a flavor focus to Indian food. Pickling can be done in vinegar or in brine. Traditional brining gives pickles probiotic qualities and are good for your health.

Pink Pickled Onions

These can be made in half an hour, are very pretty, and can be used in salads, sandwiches, or burgers as a relish. I love them so much that I eat them out of the jar and have to make more. (Photo on page 10.)

Makes a 1 pt [480 ml] jar

⅝ cup [150 ml] red wine vinegar

3 Tbsp sea salt

2 Tbsp superfine sugar

1 cup [240 ml] water

1 large red onion, finely sliced

Mix the vinegar, salt, sugar, and water, stirring to dissolve the sugar and salt. Put the onion in a sterilized 1 pt [480 ml] jar (see page 13), top with as much pickling liquid as will fit, leave for 30 minutes or so, and it will turn a hot pink color. Eat within 2 weeks.

Pickled Green Grapes

I used "sultana" grapes from my local store, which stocks Turkish food, but you can use any seedless white/green grapes. I keep a jar of these in my pantry and sling them on salads. (Photo on page 10.)

Makes a 1 pt [480 ml] jar

⅝ cup [150 ml] white wine vinegar

2 Tbsp superfine sugar

3 Tbsp coarse sea salt or sel gris

1 Tbsp mustard seeds

1 cup [240 ml] water

8¾ oz [250 g] seedless green grapes (only unbruised fruit), stems removed

Mix the vinegar, sugar, salt, mustard seeds, and water together in a medium saucepan and heat until the sugar has dissolved, then remove from the heat and let it cool. Put the grapes in a sterilized 1-pt [480-ml] jar (see page 13) and top with as much cool pickling liquid as will fit. These will keep for months.

A salsa is made of finely chopped vegetables and fruit, dressed with lemon or lime and seasoned. It is fine enough to serve as a sauce. A classic salsa contains tomatoes, onion, jalapeño, lime, and coriander. Mexican pico de gallo is very similar to salsa, with almost identical ingredients, but it is less liquid and chunkier. Make an

unusual salsa by dicing and mixing mango, scallions, and fresh ginger together and seasoning with salt.

A kachumber is a finely diced piquant salad found in Indian cookery. It is very similar to Mexican salsa, but with the addition of spices such as cumin, coriander, paprika, and chaat masala.

Chimichurri is an Argentinian relish made from parsley, garlic, olive oil, oregano, white wine vinegar, and salt, all minced together.

Sambal is a southern Indian version of a kachumber, but it is sometimes a paste; a coconut, lime and chile recipe for this is on page 82.

Oils

I like to use different oils; not just the standard olive oil for dressings, and vegetable or sunflower oil for frying.

Olive oil has a distinct flavor and the best quality should be used on food, as heating it will destroy some of its quality. Extra-virgin olive oil is new oil—that is what is meant by "virgin." It shouldn't have any mustiness or mold in the scent; it should taste and smell grassy, peppery, vital.

Sunflower oil in the US and UK is regarded as a bog-standard cooking oil, but when I visited Georgia, it was dark kelp in color, with an intense flavor. You could just dip your bread in it, like we do with olive oil.

Austria has a rich **pumpkin seed oil** that is worth trying.

Sometimes you want a neutral oil for a dish: Asian cooking uses **peanut oil** for this purpose, with **sesame oil** as a finishing touch.

I also use **walnut, hazelnut, avocado, macadamia, coconut, mustard,** or **hay-smoked canola oil.**

Do experiment with oils and vinegars, adding herbs, chile, and citrus, to introduce yet another element to plant-based cookery. Store oil in a cool, dark place; I once mistakenly kept a 5¼-qt [5-L] can of good olive oil next to my Aga stove for a couple of days and the next time I used it I ruined a whole recipe, as it was disgustingly rancid.

Nuts, Seeds & Herbs

You will be using nuts and seeds as a protein substitute for animal products. A few lightly toasted nuts and seeds are a tasty, textural garnish on salads and soups; I sling them in everything.

Nut milks are useful and quick to make. In fact, once you've made your own, you'll wonder why cows' milk is still the standard.

Dukkah is an Egyptian nut and herb mix: try it as a snack with bread and oil, or sprinkle it over dishes.

Macadamia Dukkah

Makes a small bowlful

¾ cup [100 g] macadamia nuts

1 tsp coriander seeds

½ tsp cumin seeds

2 Tbsp za'atar (a Middle Eastern herb mix with thyme)

1 tsp dried mint

Sea salt

Dry-roast the nuts and seeds in separate batches in a frying pan over medium-high heat. Let cool, then blitz with the za'atar and mint using a food processor or mortar and pestle until crumbly. Salt to taste.

Gomashio is a dry Japanese condiment. Make your own by roasting ¾ cup [50 g] black sesame seeds and then grinding with 1 tsp sea salt.

An Italian herby condiment, **gremolata** is great on asparagus, pasta, and beans. Simply blitz together the grated zest of 2 lemons, a garlic clove, and a handful of flat-leaf parsley.

A North African marinade, **chermoula** works well on grilled vegetables, couscous, and freekeh. Blitz a large bunch of fresh cilantro leaves, 1 Tbsp ground cumin, 2 Tbsp olive oil, 4 peeled garlic cloves, 1 tsp paprika, the juice of 1 lemon, and sea salt to taste in a food processor until you get a paste.

Sourdough bread crumbs can be sprinkled on your food to give texture, as well as flavor. Use them in soups and burgers, and on gratins.

Soy

One thing you are likely to start eating more of as a vegan is the humble soybean. From it you can make milk, tofu, yogurt, flour, and you can of course, eat the bean itself.

Tofu is derided by Westerners as being flavorless. It does have a subtle flavor, but its real asset is its texture and the nutrition within: lots of protein and little fat. Texturally, tofu ranges from extra firm, to medium, to silken. Extra firm to medium can be used in stir-fries, whereas silken is good for desserts or soups. Japanese silken tofu is a whole other texture, like delicate cream. I don't freeze tofu, as I don't like the texture—it goes chewy—but some people like that.

Making your own is less difficult than you might think and certainly a cheaper option; see page 33.

Coconut

Coconut is another of those all-purpose foodstuffs like the soybean. Each element of the coconut tree can be used: the leaves, the husk for coir matting, the young buds, which are hearts of palm, the shell as a receptacle, the flesh as fresh "meat" or to extract flour, oil, butter, sugar, milk, or cream, and lastly, the water as a refreshing drink. The water has on occasion been used in drips as a replacement for blood, plus it has estrogen qualities, so it's good for the menopause. It's magical stuff, and forms part of the creation myths of several cultures. If you want to avoid Alzheimer's, eating coconut can help.

How to Open a Fresh Coconut

When you buy a coconut, shake it to make sure there is still water sloshing inside. The coconut will have three "eyes," one or two of which will be softer. Pierce two of its eyes with a corkscrew or screwdriver, and upend the coconut into a glass to collect the water. Then, to crack it open, you can smash it against a concrete floor; with the back of a machete, cleaver, or heavy knife, VERY CAREFULLY tap around the "equator" line that runs around the coconut and it should just split open (this does work—I've tried it); or find a safe area without breakables, place the coconut in a plastic bag and whack it with a hammer (mind your hands).

You can buy frozen coconut flesh from Asian supermarkets, and dried, sweetened, or unsweetened coconut. When you buy coconut milk in cans, check that it is a good brand without too many thickeners.

Vinegars & Sourness

Introducing acidity into food is another way of augmenting flavor. My favorites are lemon and lime juice, but there is a whole world of vinegars to be discovered. I have dozens: red and white wine, sherry, cider, Chinese black vinegar, fruit vinegars such as raspberry or pineapple, or grain vinegars like malt or rice vinegar. Each one is matched to a certain kind of dish or a different cuisine. I also use subtler acidulents such as verjuice or orange juice, or souring agents such as pomegranate molasses or the very sour citric acid (available from Asian stores).

Chiles

The Mexicans know that every chile has a distinct flavor. You want more than just heat; you want fruit, spice, sweetness, smokiness, and differing degrees of heat. If it is difficult to get hold of interesting fresh chiles, you should still have access to dried ones, or canned chiles in the form of pickled or smoked chipotles, or in adobo sauce (really flavorsome). I like to use dried anchos or guajillos, which are mild, and dried chipotles, which are smoked dried jalapeños. The Peruvian yellow chile aji amarillo is also good and can be bought in the US fresh, as a paste, or dried.

Rarer still are genuine Scotch bonnets—mostly they are habaneros. You can tell by smell: proper Scotch bonnets have a fruity smell, whereas habaneros are just heat. I love the Italian pepperoncini: flavorsome and not too hot fresh, they also make great red pepper flakes on pizza and pasta when dried.

How to Prepare Dried Chilies

To get the maximum flavor from a dried chili, first split it open, shake out the seeds and toast it in a dry frying pan until it softens—this happens very quickly, so don't walk away. Now soak the chili in enough hot water to cover it. Reserve the liquid and scoop out the chilies, then chop them finely. Try adding soaked chipotle flakes to the Vegan Mayonnaise recipe on page 32.

Harissa is a North African chili sauce, which is lovely with the tagine on page 117, or on toast!

Pepper

Pepper is not just black and white—there is a whole range of flavors to explore.

Sichuan is a Chinese peppercorn that has a unique taste and makes your mouth tingle. In Japanese cooking, this is called sansho pepper. Use one of these instead of chiles in Asian cooking.

White pepper fell out of fashion to the big black pepper grinder for years, but for paler dishes, I love it.

Green peppercorns are young black peppercorns. I love them pickled or fresh; the latter you can buy in Asian supermarkets.

Pink pepper is not technically pepper, but a berry. It has a lovely flavor and contrasting color to dress dishes.

Long pepper looks as its name suggests, and is often used in Indian cookery.

Salt

I'm a big fan of salt—good sea salt, that is, with all the minerals, metals and nutrients, not ordinary table salt. I salt in the cooking to avoid salting at the table. This way I use less salt. There is good scientific data showing that salt does not increase blood pressure except for the 8 percent of people who have a salt sensitivity. (If using ordinary table salt, use a lot less than stated in the recipes.)

I use **rock salt** or **sel gris** for cooking, and Maldon sea salt for finishing and for sauces. Another salt you may not know about is **tempero**, a herby, large-grained salt from Brazil. I use it for my Canary Island-Style Tempero Salt-Baked Mini Potatoes on page 104.

I've smoked salt and added lemon zest, rose petals, and herbs. Nowadays you can buy specialized salts: black Indian, pink Himalayan, rusty orange, green bamboo, red volcanic Hawaiian.

Rosemary Salt

This is great in bread, and on pizzas, baked potatoes, and roast potatoes.

Makes 1 cup [200 g]

1 cup [200 g] good sea salt, such as fleur de sel or Maldon

Several sprigs of rosemary, finely chopped

Mix the salt and rosemary together and store in a clean, dry jar.

You can do this with any herb: just finely chop or process the herb in a food processor, then combine with the salt. Keep the salt in a dry jar in the fridge or in a sealed bag in the freezer.

Seaweed

The fifth taste, umami, in a sense originates from a seaweed called kombu. It's the seaweed that is used to flavor dashi, the Japanese soup stock whence umami derives. Seaweed is high in flavor and minerals such as iodine. If you buy the dried stuff for your pantry, it never goes off.

Nori are the purple/black sheets of seaweed, which can be eaten raw, but are better toasted, that you use to wrap sushi. Korean stores sell this in snack packs and I could scoff it by the sheet. Kids like it too. If you buy the sheets for sushi, sometimes it's necessary to re-toast it. Just pass it over a flame or dry-roast it in a pan very quickly—it will shrivel slightly and crisp up.

Wakame is used in miso and has a soft, minerally taste. A small pinch becomes huge. It's used in salads and soup.

Kombu, a type of kelp used to flavor dashi, the simple stock in Japanese cuisine, is not eaten, as the texture is very tough—it's just a flavoring. Use a segment ¼ to ½ in [6 to 12 cm] long to flavor broth.

Hijaki needs hydrating and cooking. It can be used in stir-fries or in tofu balls.

Carrageen or **Irish moss**, a red seaweed, has thickening qualities that make it a good replacement for gelatin when setting mousses, panna cotta, and jellies.

Dulse is a purple seaweed that you can crumble on rice, or use in bread making or in soups. It can also be used as chewing gum!

Sea lettuce, also known as glasswort, is good for baking parchment to cook things "en papillote;" it can also be fried.

A rather chic ingredient, **samphire** is often served with fish. But in the vegan diet it is good as a salty texture in quinoa salads, or steamed and topped with pumpkin seeds.

Sea kale can be steamed and used like asparagus, but it's very pungent and can be hard to get hold of.

Kelp can be used as an alternative to salt.

Flowers

I use quite a few flowers in my cookery and grow them in my garden for culinary use. Also look out for herb flowers, for instance pretty purple chive flowers, as they are like decorative versions of the herb and they taste similar. Do not eat flowers of the nightshade family (potatoes, tomatoes, eggplants, peppers), sweet pea flowers, hydrangeas, or foxgloves.

I've used the flowers of various beans, which again taste like the vegetable they come from, and also zucchini flowers. Always inspect inside flowers for creepy crawlies and worse. Other pointers: use unsprayed organic flowers. If the stamen is prominent, remove it.

Nasturtiums are peppery, good in salads, and the buds can be pickled.

Cornflowers are more of a garnish.

Cowslip petals are honey-like, good for drinks and syrups.

Hibiscus is acidic and bright red in color.

With **hollyhocks**, eat just the petals.

With perfumed, pungent **roses**, remove the white heel.

Lavender is perfumed and you can add it to sugar.

Pinks petals can be used as a garnish.

Primroses are small, yellow and slightly sweet.

Tulips can be steamed and stuffed, but remove the stamens.

Violets, ideally parma violets, can be candied.

Borage has small, purple flowers, ideal in tea or for garnish; remove the green calyx (the small green "leaves" that surround the flower.)

I've used both flower and leaves of **wild geraniums** in salads and pasta.

You can use the scented leaves from **lemon** or **rose pelargonium** plants in baking.

Day lilies—see recipe on page 160.

Elderflowers can be used for drinks and for flavoring, plus they make great fritters.

I sprinkle **marigolds** on top of salads and bread.

Cooking with Leaves

Vine, pandan, geranium (rose and lemon), fig.

Herbs

Fresh herbs add scent as well as flavor to a dish. Sweet leafy herbs include cilantro, dill, fennel, mint, basil, chervil, and tarragon. These are good for sauces, and adding later in the dish, plus for garnishing. Base-note herbs tend to be woody: bay (I love this; use it in tomato and creamy sauces), rosemary, oregano, marjoram, and thyme. These can be used at the beginning of a sauce and are not diminished by long cooking. When dried, some herbs change flavor: mint and oregano, for instance.

Sugar

Used both in sweet and savory dishes, every sugar has a specific quality and flavor and should be matched to the dish. Bakers tend to prefer cane sugar to beet sugar.

Types include: cane sugar, palm sugar, fructose, coconut palm sugar, agave nectar, date syrup, mulberry molasses, maple syrup, carob molasses, and brown rice syrup. Licorice is one of the sweetest substances on earth, and can be used in various forms; in tea, or a candied sugar version can be ground over desserts. I like to candy nuts, fruit, and vegetables as a contrasting flavor and texture (see page 24).

Pantry Vegan Stuff You Never Knew Existed

Eggs are so useful and have amazing properties: they bind, they stretch, they color, they glue, they thicken. Traditional sweet baking is fundamentally about using the qualities of eggs. It is tough to replace all of these qualities, but there are some alternatives. Some of them are familiar, but others will be new to you. You can buy "**egg replacers**," which work well in making meringues or "egg" pasta. **Ground linseed is referred to in certain vegan circles as "FLAX EGGS:" 1 Tbsp ground linseeds soaked in 2½ Tbsp water has similar binding properties to egg.** The same effect works with **chia seeds** in place of the linseed. **Arrowroot** makes things glossy. **Cornstarch** needs to be cooked out or the flavor stays. **Lotus root flour** is good. **Tapioca flour** is very textural, with a nice gloss and is often used in vegan cheese recipes. **Potato flour** is good for gluten-free people, but do not let the liquid boil. **Sago starch** is good for puddings. **Sahlab** is made from orchid roots, with a floral flavor and smell, and is used in Middle Eastern cooking. **Water chestnut flour** gives fried foods a crisp, nutty coating and is used in Asian cooking.

Dark chocolate is ostensibly vegan, but check the package, as some dark chocolate brands add powdered milk.

Vegan, plant-based alternatives to jelly and gelatin are available but do not have the mouthfeel of jelly, which melts at body temperature. **Carrageen or Irish Moss** is derived from seaweed (see page 20). **Agar-agar** is used in Asia and sets quite hard, so use sparingly.

Techniques: The Vegan Way

Vegans need to do a great deal of preparation. Arm yourself with the right equipment to make life easier: a sharp vegetable knife, a decent peeler, a julienne peeler, canner, pressure cooker, mandoline, and 2 Microplanes (fine and coarse). More expensive but essential is a good, powerful blender such as a Vitamix. Other less essential equipment would be a dehydrator, a stovetop smoker and a spiralizer for making vegetable "ribbons and noodles."

Sauerkraut

Food fermentation is when food breaks down and converts sugar to either lactic acid or alcohol. It is a bacteria, but a healthy one like penicillin, and aids in the preservation of food. Alcohol, pickles, yogurt, and sourdough are fermented foods. Eating more fermented foods will boost your immune system as it is naturally probiotic. The health benefits of fermentation are known all over the world: the Japanese macrobiotic diet encourages the consumption of pickles because they aid digestion, while in Eastern Europe, cabbage is fermented whole in barrels. You can ferment most foods and salt is the key ingredient that prevents them from rotting. Real sauerkraut takes time—it should be fermented slowly. The proportion of salt is 3 Tbsp for every 4½ lb [2 kg] of cabbage.

Makes a medium container

1 white cabbage

2 Tbsp rock salt

1 Tbsp dill seeds

1 Tbsp juniper berries

1 apple, cored and thinly sliced or grated

Remove any outer cabbage leaves that may be damaged and chop the cabbage into ribbons. Mix it with the salt, dill seeds, juniper berries, and apple in a food-grade plastic container.

Leave it for an hour, then start to "punch" the cabbage, pummeling it to make it softer. Then place a weight on top of it, such as a glass jar filled with water. Leave overnight, but every so often press down the weight. Eventually the cabbage ribbons should be covered with the saline liquid. If not, cover the cabbage with enough (ideally bottled) water.

Mix with your hands, pressing down. Cover completely and leave it for a couple of weeks. If it then has a tangy, fermented flavor, put it into sterilized jars (see page 13). If there is any white mold, just scoop that off—it's completely safe. If it hasn't yet fermented, cover it well again and leave for another week or two.

Baechu Kimchi

Kimchi is an ancient Korean sauerkraut. In Korea they have aged kimchis, and they even bury it underground in clay pots over winter so that the frost will break down the cabbage. You can eat your homemade kimchi immediately or after a day, after a week, after a year, but the longer it is left to ferment, the better tasting and the sourer it becomes.

Makes a medium container

1 cup [200 g] coarse sea salt

2 qt [2 L] cold water

2 heads of Napa cabbage

3 garlic cloves, minced

Thumb-sized piece of ginger, peeled and finely grated (I keep a stick in the freezer and grate it directly with a Microplane)

Scant 3 oz [75 g] gochugaru Korean red pepper powder (available online)

2 Tbsp superfine sugar

5 scallions, chopped into ¼-in [6-mm] slices

In a food-grade plastic container or other non-reactive container, mix the salt with the water.

Separate the cabbage leaves and place them in the salted water (you could also put the whole heads in). Make sure everything is submerged, then put a plate over the top and a glass jar filled with water on top of that. Soak for 24 hours so that the leaves become soft and pliable, then drain, rinse, and squeeze dry.

In the meantime, blend the garlic, ginger, red pepper powder, and sugar together in a food processor.

Put the drained cabbage leaves back into the plastic container in layers, spreading the chile mixture and scallions between each layer, until all the cabbage is used up.

Pack the seasoned cabbage, rolling up the leaves, into a sterilized glass mason or similar jar (see page 13), and let it ferment in a cool place for 3 days before eating.

If you want to try fermenting it for longer, check it every few days to make sure it isn't building up too much gas in the jar (just open the top of the jar a little to check).

Pickled Watermelon Rind

I've pickled walnuts, onions, cucumbers, cherries, lemons, limes, onions, and cauliflower. Pickles are good for you, with zero fat, and add zing to your food. This is a Southern-style pickle, beloved of Elvis and Dolly.

Makes two 1-pt [480-ml] jars

1 small watermelon

Scant 1 cup [200 ml] white wine vinegar

Scant ½ cup [100 ml] water

1 cup [200 g] sugar

2 Tbsp sea salt

Thumb-sized piece of ginger, peeled and chopped

1 cinnamon stick, broken in half

2 cloves

Working in segments, peel the green outer skin off the watermelon and remove the reddish pink flesh, scraping off the layer next to the skin with a spoon so that you are left with just the white part. Cut this into 1¼ in [3 cm] squares or strips.

Put the vinegar, water, sugar, salt, ginger, cinnamon, and cloves into a very large saucepan. Bring to a boil, dissolving the sugar, then add the watermelon rind. Bring to a boil again, then simmer for a minute. Remove from the heat and leave it to cool for an hour.

Ladle the watermelon rind into 2 sterilized 1-pt [480-ml] jars (see page 13). Cover the rinds with the vinegar mixture, leaving ³/₈ in [1 cm] of headroom at the top. Cover with sterilized lids and keep in the fridge overnight, then it's ready to eat the next day. It will keep for just over a week.

Candied Zucchini Strips

Another cooking and preservation method that adds variety to vegan cookery is candying. Rather than adding salt to preserve a vegetable as in pickling, one adds sugar. I like to candy citrus peel, fruits, nuts, vegetables such as beets, herbs such as angelica, and flowers such as rose petals. These zucchini strips can be added to desserts or even salads! Unusual!

Makes a small bowlful

1 cup [200 g] superfine sugar

¾ cup [180 ml] water

1 zucchini, sliced lengthwise using a mandoline

Dissolve the sugar in the water in a medium saucepan over medium heat. Once dissolved, add the zucchini strips and simmer until translucent. Remove from the heat and allow to cool. Lay the strips, spreading them out flat, on a silicone mat or sheet of baking parchment, and let them dry in a dehydrator or a very slow oven (200°F [100°C]) about an hour until crisp.

Sprouting Alfalfa

"Sprouting" means germinating seeds, which you may have done at school to grow sprouts. You can sprout alfalfa, chickpeas, lentils, mung beans, quinoa, peanuts, fenugreek seeds… What do you think bean sprouts are? The sprouts of mung beans! Top chefs love their micro-greens, tiny versions of salads, herbs, and vegetables including my favorite, tendrily delicate pea shoots. Get sprouting seeds, grains, and legumes for vibrancy and crunchiness in your diet. You can buy a special sprouting jar or create one yourself with a jam jar, a rubber band and a piece of cheesecloth. Make sure the seeds are not stale and rinse them well before starting.

1 to 2 Tbsp alfalfa seeds

Add enough seeds to cover the bottom of a jam jar in a single layer. Rinse thoroughly, then add 2 to 4 in [5 to 10 cm] water. Cover the jar with a piece of cheesecloth, secure with a rubber band and leave to soak overnight. Drain the water out through the cheesecloth lid. Add another 2 to 4 in [5 to 10 cm] water, shake, strain, cover, and leave overnight—and repeat every day for 5 to 6 days. You will have a lovely jar bursting full of nutritious sprouts.

This is the simplest technique. Other techniques include putting damp cotton balls, then a sheet of folded paper towels in the base of an empty plastic vegetable container that has holes to drain. Moisten the cotton balls and spread the seeds on top of the paper towels.

If you want to get fancy and start growing chic micro-greens, think about investing in a little perlite (available from garden centers) and cover the bottom of a plastic vegetable container with it, about ⅝ in [1.5 cm] deep. Set the container in a dish and add a little water to the dish. Cover the perlite with a layer of seeds/beans/nuts and place it somewhere light and warm. The perlite will soak up the water and nourish and hydrate the seeds. You will have usable shoots in 2 to 4 days. Scissor off the tops to harvest.

Dehydrated Kiwi Fruit

An innovative, but actually old-fashioned preserving technique that many chefs, including vegans, are using is dehydration. This is the concept behind powdered vegetable bouillon or dried soup stock, which is, fundamentally, portable soup, relied upon by sailors and explorers

and campers. You will perhaps have used sun-dried tomatoes. Modern chefs scatter dried fruit powders over desserts, and ingredients like dried beet powder are fantastic for coloring pasta and tofu. Dehydration is also the theory behind fruit leather (see page 58). You can buy a dehydrator, use the bottom oven of an Aga or a normal oven with just the light on or on its lowest setting of 140°F [60°C]. You can also use the sun to dehydrate if you live in a hot country. When dehydrating fruit, choose mature, but firm, undamaged fruits. To dehydrate vegetables, do not cook beforehand if it is something you could eat raw; if you would usually cook it, then steam the vegetable for 5 to 8 minutes before drying.

Kiwi fruit, peeled and very thinly sliced

Place the slices of kiwi in a single layer on a wire rack set over a flat baking sheet and dry out overnight or for at least 8 hours in the oven, on its lowest setting, about 140°F [60°C]. After that, keep checking every couple of hours until the slices are thin but pliable. If you want a powder, continue to dry, then grind in a food processor. Store in a dry, sealed container.

Hot-Smoked Marinated Tofu

I run a monthly supper club called The Secret Garden Club with a gardener colleague called Ms. Zia Mays. We've done several smoking workshops to teach people how to smoke. It's seen as quite a macho skill, but it isn't at all. Girls can smoke! We've come a long way baby. There are three main types of smoking: cold, hot, and tea smoked. The most complicated is cold smoking, which is how smoked salmon is created. Hot smoking is much quicker than cold; but the easiest method of all is tea smoking, as it can be done on a normal kitchen stove with an old saucepan, a steamer basket, and a lid. The tea-smoking mixture comprises loose leaf

tea, raw long-grain rice, and brown
sugar. This hot-smoked recipe comes
from Zia, and it transforms tofu into
a dark brown, savory-sweet tasty food.

Makes 14 oz [400 g]

14 oz [400 g] firm tofu, drained
   and sliced around ¼ in [6 mm]
   thick

For the marinade:

3 Tbsp soy sauce

3 Tbsp maple syrup

3 Tbsp olive oil

1 tsp sesame oil

2 tsp Dijon mustard

Mix all the marinade ingredients
together in a shallow dish. Slide
the tofu slices in, cover, and
marinate in the fridge for 4 hours
or more.

Get the hot smoker ready, then lift
the tofu pieces onto a piece of foil
on the rack and hot smoke for 30
minutes. Some find the smoky flavor
of the tofu quite strong, so you
can experiment by smoking for just
15 minutes, say, and then checking
whether the flavor is right for you.

Stock

Basic vegetable stock is necessary
in particular for soups. If you
don't have time to make your own
stock, do by all means use a good-
quality powdered stock or bouillon
cubes. But from time to time, make
the effort to prepare fresh vegetable
stock, as it tastes so much more
alive than powdered stock.

Vegetable Stock

Excellent stock can be eaten without
anything else, as a pure essence of
vegetable clear soup. It becomes a
broth when other elements are included
such as solid vegetables, rice, pasta,
or beans. You could start a couple of
days beforehand with a bowl for scraps
of other meals to use in your stock.

Makes about 2 qt [2 L]

2 to 3 Tbsp olive oil

1 to 2 large onions, unpeeled,
   chopped

1 lb [450 g] carrots, washed but
   unpeeled, chopped

1 lb [450 g] celery, chopped

3 garlic cloves, peeled

1 bay leaf

10 black peppercorns

2½ qt [2.5 L] water

2 tsp sea salt

3½ Tbsp soy sauce, tamari, Maggi
   Liquid Seasoning, or Bragg
   Liquid Aminos, or 1 Tbsp Marmite

Any vegetable scraps from other
   meals (leeks, mushrooms,
   peppers, turnips, greens,
   zucchini, fennel, celery leaves.
   The only rule is: don't use
   starchy vegetables)

Parsley, including stems

Put the oil, onions, carrots, and
celery in a large, heavy-bottomed
saucepan over medium heat and sauté
them briefly. Then add the garlic,
bay leaf, black peppercorns, and
water. Cook for 1 hour, and then
add the salt and soy or other sauce,
and the parsley. Simmer for another
30 minutes.

Using a chinois (a special conical,
fine-meshed sieve) or a sieve lined
with a piece of cheesecloth, strain

the stock into another large pan or a pitcher. Squeeze the cheesecloth to get the remaining vegetable juice into the stock (or press the vegetables down in the chinois using the back of a small ladle).

Leave the strained stock to cool, then either freeze or keep in the fridge for up to 3 days. If you want to keep it for longer, boil it up again after a couple of days, adding more vegetables. In the old days, a pot of stock would be kept constantly on the go, and as it reduced, more would be added.

Dashi

This is the vegan version of the Japanese stock that forms the basis of miso soup. Do not boil this stock.

Makes about 1 qt (1 L)

3¼ in [8 cm] square of kombu

1 qt (1 L) water

Put the kombu and water into a pan over low heat. After approximately 10 minutes, small bubbles will form and the kombu will begin to float.

Remove the kombu and bring the liquid just to a boil, then quickly take the pan off the heat and add ½ cup [120 ml] of cold water, to reduce the temperature.

Strain through a strainer lined with paper towels or cheesecloth, and use within 3 days.

How to Cook Vegetables Well

We British have a poor reputation when it comes to cooking vegetables; we boil them to death so that they end up limp, flaccid, and devoid of flavor. But I think we have learned

a thing or two over the years. Cut vegetables into even sizes and they will all cook at the same rate.

To blanch, plunge a fruit or vegetable into boiling water for a minute; this will make the skin easier to remove. If you want vegetables to retain their vivid green color, "refresh" them in ice-cold water immediately after boiling briefly in salted water. This is known as "blanch and shock." Use this technique if you want to cook ahead, or if the vegetable is denser and takes too long to sauté.

To boil, bring a pan of water to a boil on the stove before adding the vegetables. Salting the water will make it boil quicker. Try to have your vegetables in the water for as little time as possible: as soon as they are "al dente," whip them out. For green vegetables, use a large quantity of water.

To steam means to cook vegetables over boiling water using a steamer or colander and a lid to keep the steam in. This method ensures the vegetables don't become waterlogged. A tagine is a steaming method: the condensation from the water in the vegetables rises up the cone and comes down again to sit in the bottom.

Braising is very useful when cooking delicate vegetables such as asparagus; using little water means that the food does not lose its flavor or become soggy. Use a wide frying pan with a little oil and lightly fry the asparagus, then add 1 in [2.5 cm] of boiling, salted water or stock, to finish it off. To stew vegetables means to cook them for a long time in a casserole—useful for root vegetables or potatoes.

Roasting in the oven is one of my favorite methods of cooking. There is less preparation time needed: just clean the vegetables, toss them in oil and herbs in a baking pan, and let them roast in the oven on high heat. Roasting caramelizes the vegetables, and is particularly effective with root vegetables, and of course potatoes.

Sautéeing and frying are normally done over high heat on a stove, meaning that the vegetables cook quickly. Heat the pan first, then add the oil; once the oil begins to shimmer, add the vegetables. The oil should not be smoking. If it is, remove it carefully from the heat until it stops smoking and cools down. For sautéeing, fry vegetables in a shallow skillet, moving and turning with tongs or a spatula to stop them from burning. You can also deep-fry; in which case, the fat you use should generally be at 350°F to 375°F [180°C to 190°C], and make sure you submerge the vegetables in the oil. Deep-frying at the correct heat shouldn't result in greasy vegetables; in fact, the heat seals the outside, preventing the oil from entering the vegetable. This is fabulous for tempura-style vegetables: add a light batter and deep-fry. With both frying and sautéeing, do not overcrowd the pan.

Stir-frying is the Asian version of sautéeing, authentically done at such a high heat that you need water to cool down the outside of the wok. Ingredients should be already prepped, cooked quickly in order of length of cooking, so tougher vegetables go in first.

Grilling and barbecuing cause vegetables to cook on the outside first, giving a smoky, blackened, charcoal flavor. Brush oil on the outside, along with minced garlic and herbs, and grill mushrooms, peppers, tomatoes, zucchini, and eggplant.

Substitutes: Vegan DIY

You've got two choices when it comes to vegan foods: try to imitate the carnivore diet with substitutes, or develop an entirely different way of eating, less dependent on straight-up protein. Still, most vegans have been raised on a "normal" diet and from time to time crave the comforting foods they know and recognize. The following section explains the alternatives and substitutes. Some are easier than others.

Nut Milk & Cream

You will need a high-speed blender and a cheesecloth bag or gauze to make your own nut (or seed) milk and cream. You can buy inexpensive nut milk bags on Amazon or use a jelly strainer. In the fridge, the milk should last 3 to 5 days. Use in cereal or drinks, or any cooking. The cashew cream can be frozen. It's the same technique for both milk and cream—the difference is simply in the quantity of water used.

For milk (1 qt/1 L):

7 oz [200 g] almonds, cashews, hazelnuts, macadamia nuts, unsweetened coconut flakes, hemp seeds, pumpkin seeds, or sunflower seeds

3¾ cups [900 ml] water (preferably filtered or bottled to keep the taste as neutral as possible)

For sweet milk: 2 to 4 pitted dates, 1 Tbsp agave nectar, 1 tsp vanilla paste, or ¼ tsp ground cinnamon

For cream:

2½ cups [300 g] cashews

⅝ to 1¼ cups [150 to 300 ml] water, depending on how thick you want the cream

Pinch of sea salt (for savory) or 4 dates, pitted, and ½ tsp vanilla paste (for sweet)

Soak the nuts in the water for at least 2 hours, but preferably overnight. Drain the nuts and place with the water and either the savory or sweet flavoring, if using, in a powerful blender, such as a Vitamix. Whizz on high speed for 1 minute, then strain through a cheesecloth bag or a chinois into a pitcher or bottle. If it separates, just stir or shake. See Cashew, Banana, & Apricot Smoothie on page 62.

Coconut Whipped Cream

Serves 4 to 6

Two 14-fl-oz [2 x 400-ml] cans of coconut milk

¾ cup [150 g] superfine sugar

1 tsp vanilla paste

You want just the creamy part of the coconut milk, so turn the can over, open it and scoop off the hard cream, leaving the water. In a stand mixer or using an electric beater, mix the sugar and vanilla paste into the cream. Use to top any dessert, or as a side with pudding.

Thick Soy Cream

Serves 2 to 4

Scant 3 Tbsp [40 ml] sweetened soy milk

1 tsp vanilla paste

2 Tbsp agave nectar, brown rice syrup, or maple syrup

⅔ cup [160 ml] neutral oil (I prefer to use sweet cold-pressed almond oil)

Pour the soy milk into a blender, add the vanilla and syrup, then, with the motor running, slowly pour in the oil. This can also be piped.

Soy Yogurt

Of course, you can buy soy yogurt in most places now, but if you want to try making your own, here is a recipe. You will need to buy a starter soy yogurt, however.

Makes 1 qt [1 L]

1 qt [1 L] soy milk (sweetened or unsweetened)

Pinch of sea salt

2 Tbsp agar-agar or ground linseed

½ cup [120 ml] good-quality plain soy yogurt

Flavorings, if desired (fruit/berries/cinnamon)

Shake the soy milk carton and pour it into a medium saucepan. Heat over medium heat until lukewarm, then let it cool to between 100°F and 120°F [40°C and 50°C]. Whisk in the salt and agar-agar or ground linseed, to thicken.

Then add the soy yogurt, stir it in and leave it either in a covered pan in a warm place—an airing cupboard or a slow oven—or in a yogurt maker for 6 to 8 hours or overnight. Then place it in the fridge where it will thicken further. Stir in any flavorings, if desired.

After each batch, keep back ½ cup [120 ml] of the old (unflavored) yogurt in the fridge to start your next batch.

Vegan Spread

In terms of finding a butter substitute for baking, the commercial soy, sunflower, or even better, homemade vegan spread here are good choices. Coconut oil can also be used on toast. This spread requires ordering a special ingredient over the internet: liquid soy lecithin. It's relatively cheap and will last a long time, as you don't use much in the recipe. The other unusual ingredient is xanthan gum, which can often be found in the baking sections of supermarkets. People on a gluten-free diet use it for baking, as it adds stretchiness. Once you have these two ingredients, this recipe is easy, and it tastes really good. Being made of coconut oil, it's also very good for you and not too processed. Instead of adding salt, you can add another flavoring of your choice, such as Marmite or nutritional yeast, or you can add minced garlic with the salt.

Makes 9 oz [250 g]

1 tsp cider vinegar

⅔ cup [160 ml] unsweetened soy milk

¾ cup [160 g] organic coconut oil

1 tsp canola oil

1 tsp liquid soy lecithin

¼ tsp xanthan gum

1 tsp Maldon sea salt

Add the cider vinegar to the soy milk and let it curdle for about 30 seconds. Melt the coconut oil until just liquid, but not hot, in 15-second bursts in a microwave or in a saucepan on the stove. It's important not to let it get too hot.

Put the melted coconut oil and canola oil in a food processor. Process for a few seconds to make sure it is smooth, then pour in the curdled soy milk, the liquid lecithin, and the xanthan gum. Process for a minute until it is a smooth, yellow grease. Add the sea salt and mix well, then scrape using a rubber spatula into a small bowl or plastic container. Keep in the fridge for up to about 3 weeks. Great on toast.

Basic Nut Butter

Nut butters are easy to make if you have a good food processor. Just place your chosen seeds or nuts inside and process at high speed.

Suggestions

Seeds: pumpkin, sunflower, sesame (for tahini), linseed, or a mix.

Nuts: almonds, cashews, macadamia, brazil, pistachios, pecans, walnuts, peanuts (see overleaf), unsweetened coconut flakes.

Flavorings: fruit, maple syrup, cinnamon, salt, vanilla or chocolate for "Nutella." You could also sweeten butters with fruit, as in almond and apple butter or maple syrup, or with a spice, as in walnut and cinnamon butter.

If the seeds or nuts are lightly roasted beforehand, they are easier to blend into a creamy paste. If using raw, you may need to add some good-quality oil to get spreadability (coconut, walnut or flax oil, for instance). If using a blender or Vitamix, you will also need to add oil.

Peanut Butter

Makes a 7-oz [200-g] jar

7 oz [200 g] peanuts, raw or
    roasted

2 Tbsp cold-pressed oil

½ to 1 tsp sea salt

If you want to roast raw nuts (which
brings out the oils), preheat your
oven to 350°F [180°C]. Spread the
nuts in a single layer on a baking
sheet and bake for 10 minutes, or
until lightly golden. Then continue
with the rest of the recipe while
the nuts are still warm.

To make both raw and roasted nut
butter, put the nuts in a high-
speed blender or food processor.
Pulse a couple of times in 30-second
intervals, scraping down between
pulses. Then add the oil and salt.
Pulse again until smooth, unless
you want chunky peanut butter. You
can store this in a jar or plastic
container in the fridge for at least
a month.

Vegan Mayonnaise

**This basic "vegannaise" recipe can be
flavored any which way: suggestions
below. I've had non-vegan friends
try this, and they prefer it to real
mayonnaise. It's good on avocado, in
salad, on everything.**

Makes 2 cups [500 g]

1 cup [250 ml] soy milk

1 cup [250 ml] olive or canola oil

2 Tbsp cider vinegar

A squeeze of lemon juice

Sea salt

Put the soy milk in a blender, and
with the motor running, add the oil
very slowly in a stream. Then add

the vinegar and lemon juice and
you'll see the mixture coagulate
instantly. Season with salt and add
a flavoring, if you like (see below).
Put in a jar and refrigerate.

You could also treat this as a vegan
Provençal aïoli by adding a couple
of cloves of minced garlic and using
it as a sauce with lightly cooked
florets of cauliflower, green beans,
green olives, and potatoes *à la
vapeur* (boiled) with salt and a
bay leaf.

Suggested flavorings: mustard,
chipotle chiles, garlic.

Basic Nut "Cheez"

**If you've had real dairy cheese any
time recently, you're going to find it
hard to forget what it tastes like.
And in that frame of mind, any non-
dairy substitute is going to be rather
disappointing. On this basis, I must
admit I was cynical about this, but
it was delicious and I couldn't stop
eating it. It's equivalent to a soft
goat cheese or cream cheese.**

Makes about 10½ oz [300 g]

Heaping ¾ cup [100 g] macadamia
    nuts

¾ cup [100 g] cashew nuts

About 1 tsp sea salt

Flavoring, such as herbs,
    spices, or chile

Soak all the nuts overnight, then
drain off the excess water. Blend
in a powerful blender, adding salt
and any flavoring. Then transfer
the mixture to a cheesecloth-lined
strainer set over a bowl, or a
nut bag. Wrap the mixture with the
cheesecloth, press it down and leave
weighted with a jar filled with water
for 24 hours. Then serve! Great
on crackers.

Smoky Chipotle Cashew Cheese

This is a firmer-textured cheese, a bit like a Gouda perhaps, and with a deep, smoky flavor.

Makes 6 small cheeses

2½ cups [300 g] raw (unroasted) cashew nuts

6 sun-dried tomatoes, snipped into small pieces (optional)

Vegetable or olive oil spray

½ cup [50 g] nutritional yeast

6 Tbsp organic coconut oil

1 Tbsp white miso

1 Tbsp cider vinegar

1 tsp sea salt

1 tsp mustard powder

½ tsp smoked paprika

2 Tbsp liquid smoke

1 Tbsp chipotle paste

Soak the cashews in cold water overnight with the sun-dried tomato pieces, if using, then drain. Spray 6 ramekins with oil.

In a blender, pulse the drained cashews and sun-dried tomatoes, if using, with all the remaining ingredients. You can add a couple of tablespoons of warm water to the blender if you feel the mixture is too stiff.

Using a rubber spatula, scrape the "cheese" mixture into the prepared ramekins. Store in the fridge. Upend the ramekins, flipping out the cheeses, when you want to use them.

Block Tofu & Soy Milk

You will need to buy a coagulant. I recommend "nigari" crystals, which can be bought online. You can also use sodium chloride, Epsom salts, or lemon juice, but in my tests, nigari was the best. I also invested in a plastic tofu mold, although you can use ordinary kitchenware; for instance, a plastic Tupperware-style box with holes punched in the bottom, to achieve a similar effect. You will also need a cheesecloth square and a metal strainer.

Makes 1¾ lb [800 g] block of tofu

3¼ cups [500 g] dried soybeans

2½ Tbsp nigari coagulant (I used crystals)

Firstly, soak the soybeans overnight (for at least 8 hours) in a large bowl, covered with cold water. They start out as little round pellets, but as they expand, they become bean shaped.

Put 2½ qt [2.5 L] fresh water into the largest saucepan you have and place over medium heat to start warming up.

Meanwhile, drain the beans and grind with 1 qt [1 L] fresh water in a powerful blender or Vitamix. You'll probably have to do this in 2 batches. Add the finely ground bean mixture to the pan and heat until it reaches a temperature of around 160°F [70°C].

Then take a cup of the water-bean mixture from the pan and add it to the blender to rinse out the rest of the beans. Pour this into the pan and heat for around 10 minutes, taking care not to scorch the bottom of the pan.

Put a piece of cheesecloth into a metal strainer set over a bowl. Pour enough of the bean mixture to fill the strainer and press down. When you have squeezed most of the soy milk out of the mixture, you will be left with the soybean lees, also known as okara, which can be used in baking, or to make burgers.

Empty the cheesecloth of okara into a clean bowl. Keep straining, squeezing, and setting aside the okara until all the contents of your large saucepan have been emptied. You will now have soy milk in your bowl (and may need to use an extra bowl or pitcher to contain it), which you can use for your tofu, or remove some for use in tea, coffee, or smoothies. You can stop at this stage if all you want is soy milk.

Now take the okara in batches, place it back in the cheesecloth, tie the top together, and squeeze a second pressing of milk out of the beans. This pressing is important because it gets the last remnants of thick milk from the beans. You'll need another bowl at this point, to put the exhausted beans in. Continue until you have pressed all of the okara a second time.

Now put all of the soy milk, first and second pressing, back into the large saucepan. Heat gently until it reaches 160°F to 175°F [70°C to 80°C]; no hotter. This is the point where you can add flavoring, such as citrus zest, yuzu paste or sesame seeds, beet powder or finely chopped herbs such as basil or cilantro, or herb oil, if you so choose.

Once it has reached the temperature required, take it off the heat and add the nigari, which will coagulate the mixture. You don't want to add too much because the coagulants can make the tofu taste bitter, although once your tofu is formed, you can gently rinse it to get rid of any lingering bitterness.

Put a lid on the pan and wait 10 minutes, after which the soy milk will have separated into curds and whey, just as if you were making dairy cheese.

Rinse out the cheesecloth and place it in the tofu mold (see introduction). Using a slotted ladle, carefully scoop out some curds and place them in the lined mold. Continue with the remaining curds. You can discard the whey but there are uses for it—you could give it to plants! Cover the top of the tofu with the cheesecloth.

Finally, you need to press the tofu to get a compact block. If you have a dedicated tofu mold, you can put it in the press that comes with it and weigh it down with cans of food. Otherwise, use a Tupperware container or a colander and place a small plate and some cans on top to weigh it down.

After 30 minutes, gently rinse the tofu in cold water, by pouring a few cups of water on it rather than running the faucet directly on the tofu, especially if it is very delicate, or it will break up. Keep the rinsed tofu in a container of cold water in the fridge. It will keep for up to 7 days, but do change the water every day or so.

The Color Wheel of Food

Part of the balanced diet is thinking not just in terms of flavor, but of color, both contrasting and complementary. "Eat your greens" is not just a phrase meted out by concerned parents; it's based on fact: green food, particularly dark green leafy vegetables, is good for you. In Chinese medicine, there are links between the organs, taste, and color.

Consumers buy food based on its color: it is no coincidence that supermarkets use pink light on meat to make it look healthier and brighter. When eating, try to develop what some people call "rainbow" eating, i.e., working your way through a variety of colors during the course of the day to ensure you are eating a varied mix of nutrients.

We are acutely sensitive to the color of our food, so this is a little exploration of the color wheel from a health and vitamin point of view.

Black

There are no truly black foods, except for grapes and olives perhaps; most "black" foods tend to be dark purple.

Purple, violet, or mauve is a royal color, a biblical hue, a rare and expensive dye prior to synthetic dyes. Sumptuary laws prevented commoners from wearing it. Lately it has become associated with women's suffrage and feminism. Dark foods contain anthocyanins; good for eye health, anti-aging, and protecting against cancer and high blood pressure.

Blackberries, Peruvian potatoes, plums, blueberries, eggplant, purple sprouting broccoli, grapes, lavender, beets, purple yams, figs, red cabbage.

Brown

Brown is the color of the earth, often grown under the ground. Brown signifies natural, unbleached, unprocessed, real, rustic. I've included legumes here because they are dried vegetables.

Roots, turnips, rutabagas, potatoes, mushrooms, nuts, wheat, lentils, chickpeas, mung beans, onions, yams.

Green

Green used to be the color of sex rather than red, but symbolizes growth, renewal, youth, fertility, money, land, nature, spring. Mary Magdalene wears green in art, while the Virgin Mary wears blue, the color of heaven. Green is now associated with conservation and ecology; morality. You could say this color has had all the fun drained out of it. What a shame.

Good for the liver and detoxing; anti Alzheimer's; the darker the better. Contains chlorophyll, apigenin, luteolin and isothiocyanates.

Dark Green

Kale, Tuscan black cabbage, broccoli, spinach, watercress.

Medium Green

Artichokes, green lentils, snow peas, limes, runner beans, bok choy, corn salad, arugula, chives, scallions, kiwi fruit, apples, gooseberries, grapes, green tea, wasabi, capers.

Knowledge is Power

Light Green

Lettuce, peas, Brussels sprouts, cabbage, Napa cabbage, green gage plums, chayote squash, leeks, zucchini, chicory, tomatillos, herbs, avocados, cucumber, snow peas, celery, mustard cress, asparagus.

Red

Red signifies ripeness, heat, energy, the ability to fight. Anti-cancer properties, cardiovascular conditions, contains resveratrol, an element of the "French Paradox" (in which French people who drink red wine have lower incidences of heart disease), lycopene (anti-prostate cancer) and capsaicin, which gives you a natural high.

Peppers, tomatoes, chiles, beets, red cabbage, strawberries, apples, watermelons, radishes, rhubarb, raspberries, red onions, pomegranates, cranberries, cherries, red wine.

Orange to Yellow

Orange signifies sunshine, optimism, summer, gold.

Contains carotenoids, good for skin health and elasticity, healthy bones and stomach. Many fruits are in the yellow to red spectrum including vegetables that are botanically fruit such as tomatoes, peppers, and pumpkins. Citrus contains limonoids, an anti-cancer agent, so grate lemon zest onto everything.

Sweet potatoes, carrots (containing alpha carotene, which the body processes into vitamin A), corn (lutein and zeaxanthin benefit eyesight), pumpkins/squash and squash blossoms, turmeric root (contains curcumin, an antioxidant and anti-fat), persimmons, oranges, mandarins, tangerines, clementines, kumquats (contain beta-cryptoxanthin, good for eyesight and healthy bones), pineapple and papaya (contain bromelain, an anti-inflammatory), grapefruit, lemons, melon, mangoes, apricots, peaches, nectarines, parsnips, bananas, rutabagas, passion fruit, cape gooseberry or physalis, jackfruit, quince.

White

White is associated with wealth, purity, and being rich enough not to work outdoors. Rich people ate white bread and white sugar in the past, and the poor tried to emulate them. Now rich people eat brown bread! White food is often bleached and therefore has fewer vitamins. Good for the immune system, and possesses diuretic properties.

Lima beans, cauliflower, celeriac, asparagus, mushrooms, potatoes, soybeans, garlic, daikon radishes, parsnips, salsify, coconuts.

Forced rhubarb and forced endive are paler than their "unforced" versions. The lack of light means they are ivory colored and tender.

The missing color is blue. One of the few true blue foods is blue corn. Hence in professional kitchens the band-aids (and paper towels) are blue, because you can easily pick them out if they drop in the food.

Snacks

Vegans, like everybody else, get hungry when they are on the move, but vegan fast food is not always readily available. Naturally there is the old standby: fruit and nuts. We all love to snack between meals, and while the French may say this is not a good thing, it's especially important for vegans to have a few energy boosters to stave off low blood sugar. This is probably one of the most important chapters of this book. Having a few snacks that you know how to make quickly and easily, as opposed to lengthier meals with lots of prep, is essential. Some of these can be made in advance for lunchboxes and pick-me-ups.

13 Things on Toast

Of course, I'm a Marmite lover, which is vegan, and I grew up with Marmite on toast for breakfast. My whole family are toast fiends. Toast is more than breakfast—it's an all-day thing. It's an all-night thing too. If I can't sleep, I get up and make toast. Yes, I have crumbs in my bed.

For each "recipe" below, spread the contents on in the given order, starting with good bread, toasted or otherwise, or oatcakes, or rice cakes, or whatever! Each "recipe" serves one and will top 2 slices of toast, or bread in the case of Number 3.

1 Strawberries, balsamic vinegar, black pepper

Coconut oil or vegan cream cheese

4 to 5 strawberries, sliced

Balsamic vinegar, for drizzling

Black pepper

2 White miso, radishes, dill

2 Tbsp white miso

4 to 5 radishes, thinly sliced

A few fronds of dill

3 Olive oil, brown sugar

2 slices of bread

Big slug of good olive oil

3 Tbsp brown sugar

4 Cinnamon toast

Broil one side of the bread, then add the toppings and broil the other side to caramelize the sugar.

Coconut oil or vegan spread

1 to 2 Tbsp ground cinnamon

1 to 2 Tbsp brown sugar

5 Dark chocolate spread, hazelnuts

4 Tbsp vegan dark chocolate spread

Scattering of chopped toasted hazelnuts

A little sea salt

6 Black or green tapenade

(This is also a good canapé)

4 Tbsp black or green tapenade

½ lemon, thinly sliced

7 The healthy Elvis

Peanut butter

1 banana, sliced or mashed

Drizzle of maple syrup

8 Marmite, tahini, alfalfa sprouts

Coconut oil or vegan spread

Marmite

Tahini

Alfalfa sprouts

9 Peanut butter, red chili jam

3 Tbsp crunchy peanut butter

2 Tbsp red chili jam

10 Avocado, chili

1 ripe avocado

Squeeze of lime juice

Scattering of dried red pepper flakes

11 Tomatoes, garlic, olive oil

1 garlic clove, to rub on the toast

2 medium tomatoes, thinly sliced

Olive oil, for drizzling

Sea salt and freshly ground pepper

Small handful of basil leaves, to garnish

12 Tahini, maple, or date syrup

Similar principle to the olive oil/brown sugar combo: the fudgy nuttiness of tahini is a lovely counterpoint to either maple or date syrup.

2 Tbsp tahini

2 Tbsp maple or date syrup

13 Spicy cashew cheese

4 Tbsp Smoky Chipotle Cashew Cheese (see page 33)

A few slices of fresh red chile (optional)

Sushi Rice

Although Japanese food is known for its fresh fish, it's easy to make vegan sushi. Sushi and onigiri (below) are treated as snack food in Japan. I think they are the perfect plane food. (If you are traveling, another option is to order the Asian meal, which is usually vegan and pretty good.)

It is awkward making sushi, but keep practicing. I had a Japanese cookery lesson with Hiromi Stone and she emphasized the importance of fresh "new season" rice, so check the dates on the package! She prefers Californian sushi rice rather than Italian, as it is better quality. Authentic Japanese sushi rice is quite expensive.

Heaping 1½ cups [300 g] sushi rice

1½ cups [360 ml] water

1 tsp sea salt

⅓ cup [80 ml] rice vinegar

Rinse the rice in a strainer. Repeat at least 3 times until the water runs clear. Put the rice and water in a medium saucepan, cover, and place over high heat until the water boils, then turn it down to a simmer and add the salt. Cook, covered, for 15 to 20 minutes, then remove from the heat and allow to steam for 10 to 15 minutes, still covered.

Transfer the rice to a shallow, wide bowl and "fold" it using a wooden spoon or spatula; you are trying to cool down the rice (the Japanese use a fan) and stirring will give it a shine. Add the vinegar and continue to fold the rice until it is cool enough to handle. Do not refrigerate the rice before using in the Onigiri Rice Triangles, as it will go hard.

Onigiri Rice Triangles

Warm cooked sushi rice
  (see above)

Small squares or strips
  of nori seaweed

Sea salt

Suggested fillings:

Umeboshi plums, pitted,
  or umeboshi paste

Shredded carrot or cucumber,
  mixed with a little soy
  sauce

Japanese pickles, such as
  ginger or daikon radish

Have a bowl of warm water nearby when you're assembling these to prevent the rice sticking to your hands.

Wet your hands and put a little salt in the palm of your left hand. Grasp about ½ cup of rice and place it in the palm of the same hand. Make a small well in the centre, place your chosen filling in the well and cover with more rice. Gently but firmly shape into a pyramid, turning as you shape. Wrap with the nori, adding a dab of the filling to the outside for identification purposes. Wrap in plastic wrap, if eating on the run!

Crispy Black Cabbage or Kale Chips

**Serves 1 person
(with self-restraint)**

Approx. 3 to 4 large
leaves of black
cabbage or kale per
baking sheet, washed
and dried

Generous glug of olive
or nut oil, such as
walnut or avocado

Option 1:

1 heaping Tbsp almond
butter

1 Tbsp sea salt

Sprinkling of dulse
(purple seaweed) and/
or bright green sea
lettuce

Option 2:

1 Tbsp nutritional
yeast

1 tsp sea salt

I don't even like kale, but these are very addictive.
Turns out that Gwyneth Paltrow knows what she is
talking about. Two versions here. I used black cabbage
which is similar, as I have plenty of it growing in
the garden. It is a fantastic way of making kids eat
greens too. I would do at least 3 baking sheets of
these at a time as you get through them very quickly.
(Photo on page 40.)

Preheat the oven to 350°F [180°C]. Strip the
leaves either side of the bitter stalk and then
tear again into roughly 1¼ in [3 cm] square
sections. Lay them on foil or baking parchment
in a single layer on baking sheets.

Option 1: Mix the oil, almond butter, and salt
together in a small bowl, then rub the mixture
into the leaves. Bake for about 10 minutes until
crispy, then top with the purple dulse or green
sea lettuce.

Option 2: Mix the oil, nutritional yeast, and
salt together, then rub the mixture thoroughly
into the leaves, making sure every bit is
covered. Bake for about 10 minutes until crispy.

Vegan Malt Loaf

Makes 1 large loaf

3 Tbsp malt extract
(available online and
in pharmacies)

Scant ½ cup [100 ml]
light corn syrup

Scant ½ cup [100 ml]
date syrup

Generous ½ cup [130 ml]
soy milk

¾ cup (about 18) dates,
pitted

1¾ cups [225 g] self-
rising flour

Pinch of sea salt

This is a really fudgy, gooey, rich recipe that works
well with the Roasted Carrot Dip on page 52. Malt
extract contains lots of iron and vitamins. (Photo on
page 48.)

Preheat the oven to 375°F [190°C]. Grease and
line a large 9-by-5-in [1-kg] loaf pan.

Warm the malt extract, light corn syrup,
date syrup, and soy milk together in a large
saucepan, then fold in the dates, flour,
and salt.

Transfer the mixture to the prepared loaf pan
and bake for 40 minutes.

45

Nine Dips, and the Rise of Hummus

If you are a vegetarian or vegan, you are bound to have a hummus recipe already. Over the last decade, hummus has become the go-to health food; its share of the market is booming. I remember when supermarkets first started selling hummus. It was beige, quite textural, and not that nice. It used to be hippie food, earnest stuff that you bought in 70s vegetarian restaurants. It was also the brown puddle next to the pink puddle in Greek restaurants.

Since then, it has improved, to the point that the average supermarket sells tons of it. There are shelves dedicated to hummus: plain, organic, lemon and cilantro, jalapeño, red pepper, avocado. Is there anything that hummus doesn't go with? (Actually there is; I once had a posh meal at a London hotel where they served fish on a bed of hot hummus. Truly horrible.)

This dip has become the healthy food for kids' lunchboxes, the standby snack for tired chefs, a vegan staple and loved by Arabs, Israelis, activists, and prime ministers.

How many times a day can you eat hummus? In Israel, approximately four times a day and definitely with every meal. "Hummus" means "chickpea" in Arabic.

While hummus is so ancient that it is mentioned in the Bible, there is controversy over its cultural appropriation, for Israelis are accused of marketing it as an Israeli product (along with falafel). But let's face it, almost every recipe on the planet is stolen. The story of recipes throughout the world and throughout history boils down to: I like the taste of that, show me how to make it. Then the "thief" gives the dish some tweaks.

On a visit to Israel, I visited the Strauss factory where they make Sabras hummus, the most popular brand in the United States. "It's all about the garnish," said Ofra Strauss, the president. "In the UK you don't really 'do' garnishes. Also, your hummus is not cooked; it's quite rough. In the States they prefer smooth cooked hummus, which is pasteurized, and they like to have garnishes. Artichokes are one of the most popular toppings." They eat hummus in every part of the US, but the highest concentration is in Boston, where it is scoffed in industrial quantities by students.

One of the food developers at the Strauss factory, when I asked about the differences between Israeli hummus and that of their Arab neighbours, said that hummus in Israel (and Lebanon) has a higher percentage of tahini (25%), less lemon, less spice, and less seasoning. This is a general rule with food, he said—there is less spice and seasoning when the country of origin is wealthy, while food is spicier and more flavored in poorer, more southern countries, with a higher pH (acidity/lemon). Personally, I prefer less tahini and more spice. I'm a peasant when it comes to food.

There are 101 things you can do with hummus, but you can also make dips from other legumes: fava beans, ful medames, lentils... Or in any of the ways on the following pages. Everyone loves dips—they're grown-up baby food.

1 My Basic Hummus

Serves 4 to 6

¾ cup [125 g] dried chickpeas (garbanzo beans) + ½ Tbsp baking soda, plus a pinch; or 14 oz [400 g] can/jar of chickpeas from India

2 Tbsp tahini

Juice of ½ lemon

1 Tbsp ground cumin

1 tsp ground coriander

Generous glug of good olive oil

1 garlic clove

Good sea salt

To garnish:

Chickpeas and/or toasted pine nuts

Paprika

Chopped parsley

If using dried chickpeas (garbanzo beans), soak them overnight in plenty of cold water with the baking soda, then drain and rinse. Place in a large pan, cover with water, and add a pinch of salt and another pinch of baking soda (not too much, as you want the softening qualities without the soapy flavor). Cook for 2 hours or until soft, topping up the water if necessary to keep them covered. (If you live in an area with soft water, the cooking time may be less. It also depends on the freshness—yes, even of dried chickpeas—and the type of chickpeas.) Once soft, drain and leave to cool.

Whizz the cooked or drained canned chickpeas, the tahini, lemon juice, cumin, coriander, and olive oil together in a food processor or blender. Crush the garlic with at least 1 Tbsp salt and add. Taste. You may need more lemon juice. Play around with seasonings. Top with the garnishes and eat with warm flatbread, such as pita.

2 Ful Medames Dip

Serves 4 to 6

1 scant cup [100 g] dried fava beans or 14-oz [400-g] can of fava beans

2 Tbsp tahini

2 Tbsp olive oil, plus extra to garnish

Juice of 1 lemon

1 garlic clove, crushed

1 tsp smoked paprika

Sea salt, to taste

Handful of parsley

"Ful" are dried fava beans, a legume made infamous by Hannibal the Cannibal. You can make this Egyptian dip with fresh or frozen fava beans too. Think of it as a funkier, sludgier hummus.

If using dried beans, boil them in water for 30 to 40 minutes (no need to pre-soak), then drain. Otherwise, drain the can. Add the beans, tahini, oil, lemon juice, garlic, paprika, and some salt to a food processor. Whizz to combine (or mash everything by hand), then transfer to a bowl, drizzle over more olive oil, and sprinkle with parsley.

47

(3) Skordalia

Serves 4 to 6

18 oz [500 g]
  Cypriot potatoes,
  peeled and diced

2 to 3 garlic
  cloves, crushed

¼ to ⅓ cup [50 to
  100 ml] olive oil

Juice of 1 lemon

Sea salt

For the garnish:

Handful of mint,
  finely chopped

Handful of flat-leaf
  parsley, finely
  chopped

Handful of walnuts,
  finely chopped
  (optional)

Olive oil, lemon
  juice and sea salt

Cypriot potatoes—waxy, red-skinned, firm-fleshed—are one of the best to make skordalia. Classically Cypriot, this dip sounds rather unglamorous on the page, consisting of cold mashed potatoes, but it's actually very addictive. This is easier if you have a food processor, as it's got to be as silky as a baby's bottom; lumps would ruin it. In the absence of Cypriot potatoes, use any waxy ones.

Put the potatoes into a pan of salted cold water and bring to a boil. Boil for 10 minutes, then drain. Put the garlic, half the potatoes, and half the olive oil in a food processor and process until smooth.

Dissolve 1 Tbsp salt, or to taste, in the lemon juice, in a pitcher. Mix the rest of the olive oil into the juice, whisking thoroughly. Add this liquid and the rest of the cooked potatoes to the food processor and process until smooth. Check for seasoning and leave to cool.

For the garnish, mix the herbs and walnuts, if using, with olive oil, lemon juice, and salt to taste. Top the skordalia with the garnish and eat with bread, pita, batons of raw veg, or fried strips of zucchini, red pepper, and eggplant.

(4) Yellow Pepper Dip with Walnuts

Serves 4 to 6

2 yellow bell peppers, roasted, skinned
  and seeded (see opposite)

Handful of walnuts, plus extra,
  chopped, to garnish

Juice of 1 lemon or lime

2 garlic cloves, minced

1 to 2 Tbsp good sunflower or pumpkin seed
  oil, plus extra to garnish

Tiny pinch of saffron strands

1 Tbsp Maldon sea salt

Blend the roasted peppers, walnuts, juice, garlic, and oil in a food processor. Grind the saffron and sea salt with a mortar and pestle. Combine with the blended ingredients in a bowl and garnish with the walnuts and a drizzle of oil.

5 Red Pepper Dip with Sesame Crostini

Serves 4 to 6

4 red bell peppers

1 red chile

1 to 2 Tbsp good olive oil, plus extra for roasting

Juice of 1 lemon

2 garlic cloves, minced

½ tsp ground cumin

½ tsp ground coriander

1 Tbsp Maldon sea salt

Slivered pistachio nuts, to garnish (optional)

For the crostini:

½ baguette or ciabatta, thinly sliced into rounds

Olive oil, for drizzling

Sea salt, for sprinkling

3 Tbsp sesame seeds (white or black)

This is a bit like muhammara but even simpler. It takes minutes. I've only put one chile in, which gives you residual heat without blowing your head off. Seed the chile if you don't want too much heat.

Preheat the oven to 400°F [200°C]. Roast the peppers and chile on an oiled baking sheet for 20 minutes for the peppers, and 10 minutes for the chile.

Strip the skin off the peppers and chile while they are still hot and steamy—much quicker and easier. Discard the seeds and the stems. Whizz the flesh in a blender with the rest of the ingredients except the pistachios. Remove to a bowl and leave to cool.

For the crostini, preheat the oven to 400°F [200°C](or keep it hot after roasting the peppers and chile). Grease a baking sheet with olive oil and place the bread rounds on the sheet. Drizzle the tops with olive oil, and scatter with salt and the sesame seeds. Bake for 5 minutes or until lightly golden, then flip and bake for another 2 minutes.

6 Guacamole

Serves 2 to 4

2 ripe Hass avocados

1 jalapeño chile, roasted, skinned, and seeded (see recipe above for roasting), then finely chopped

1 small red onion, finely diced

Juice of 1 lime

½ tsp ground cumin

Handful of cilantro, finely chopped

Sea salt, such as fleur de sel or Maldon

I make this very simply, the way Mexicans do. No garlic. NO GARLIC. Got it?

Peel, halve, and pit the avocados. Chop into cubes, then roughly mash with a fork to make a chunky paste. Don't use a blender or food processor; you want it slightly rough, not whipped like a storebought guacamole. Stir in the chile, onion, lime juice, cumin, 1 Tbsp salt, and the cilantro. Taste and season with salt.

7 Roasted Carrot Dip

Serves 4 to 6

6 large, crunchy, sweet carrots, topped, tailed, and pared

2 to 3 garlic cloves, unpeeled

3 Tbsp olive oil, plus extra for roasting

2 Tbsp agave nectar

1 Tbsp coriander seeds

Juice of ½ lemon

Sea salt

For the garnish:

Organic cold-pressed pumpkin seed oil (the dark petrol-green Styrian oil from Austria is excellent)

Pomegranate or date syrup, or cilantro leaves

This makes a good lunch option with the Vegan Malt Loaf (see page 45).

Preheat your oven to 400°F [200°C] and toss the carrots and garlic cloves (in their skins) in some olive oil. Spread out in a roasting pan and roast for 15 to 20 minutes, then remove from the oven, slip the garlic cloves from their skins and leave to cool.

Put the carrots, garlic, olive oil, agave nectar, coriander seeds, lemon juice, and salt to taste in a powerful blender or Vitamix and process until smooth (you can leave it as a rougher texture if you prefer). Drizzle and/or sprinkle over the garnish ingredients to serve.

8 Soy Tzatziki Dip

Serves 4 to 6

Maldon sea salt or other good flaky sea salt

1 cucumber, peeled (seeded if it's not good quality) and thinly sliced

1¼ cups [300 ml] plain soy yogurt

2 Tbsp dried mint or—Indian trick, this—mint sauce in a jar, or fresh herbs such as mint (traditional), cilantro, dill, parsley or tarragon (very Georgian)

Juice of 1 lemon

Fresh mint leaves, to garnish

So many cultures have a refreshing yogurty dip: raita for the Indians, tzatziki for the Greeks. Call it what you like, I love this stuff and can eat it for breakfast, in bed, lunch, or dinner.

Mix 1 Tbsp salt with the cucumber slices and set aside for 30 minutes or longer, then pour away the liquid released. This is a French tip I learned to make the cucumber crunchy.

Add the soy yogurt, dried mint or other herbs, and the lemon juice, and mix together. Adjust the seasoning if necessary, and garnish with fresh mint.

9 Baba Ghanoush

Serves 4 to 6

3 large, shiny
eggplants

1 heaping Tbsp
tahini

Juice of 1 lemon

2 garlic cloves,
minced

1 tsp ground
cumin

2 Tbsp good
olive oil

2 Tbsp Maldon
sea salt

Pomegranate
seeds or
chopped
parsley,
to garnish

I make the best baba ghanoush in the world. Yes, I'm boasting, but it's the truth. In fact, I challenge anyone in the entire world to a baba ghanoush-off. No kidding.

Char the eggplants on a gas stove, either directly on the flame, or in a flat cast-iron pan, or alternatively, under the broiler or on a barbecue. (You can even perch a disposable barbecue on your windowsill. Try not to drop it onto someone's head below.) If you don't like any of those options, roast them in the oven at 375°F [190°C] for 20 to 30 minutes until the skin is blackened and the eggplants look shrunken inside. I insist upon this charring process because that's what this dish is all about—the smoky burnt taste from the eggplants. Always include a little bit (a couple of inches) of the charred skin in the dip.

Strip the skin off the eggplants, discard the stems and put the flesh in a blender with a little of the charred skin. Add the other ingredients except the garnish, blend, keep tasting and adjust it to your taste. That's fine, you can. I'm not a food deity. You like less salt? Fine. You like more? Go ahead.

Serve topped with the pomegranate seeds or parsley.

Nut & Seed Mix

Makes a small bowlful

2 sheets of nori
seaweed

3 Tbsp each
[25 g] pumpkin
seeds, sunflower
seeds, and
sesame seeds

1 heaping Tbsp
[10 g] flaxseeds

1½ Tbsp [10 g]
hemp seeds

2 Tbsp tamari
sauce

My daughter loves this. It was a standard recipe throughout her childhood, one of the few "healthy" things I could get her to eat. Carry it around in a little sealed bag or sprinkle it over other foods.

Dry-roast the nori sheets in a skillet for just 5 seconds; you don't want them to start to shrivel. Set aside. Dry-roast all the seeds in the pan, starting with the largest; the pumpkin seeds. Now add the tamari to the pan and stir to coat the nuts and seeds. Crumble in the nori. Keep in a dry, airtight container for weeks.

Cheesy Popcorn

Makes a bowlful

1 movie or a binge-
    watch of a Netflix
    series

Olive or coconut oil

An unspecified amount
    of popping corn

3 Tbsp nutritional
    yeast

Sea salt

Optional extras:

Sprinkle over some
    seaweed, such
    as dulse or sea
    lettuce

Crumble over some
    Crispy Black
    Cabbage or Kale
    Chips (see
    page 45)

Crumble over some
    toasted nori
    seaweed and black
    sesame seeds

Variations:

Did you know you can
pop grains other than
corn? Try popquinoa,
popamaranth (for this
one do not add oil to
the pan), popbulgur,
popbarley, popwildrice
and popsorghum.
However, these grains
do not expand as much
as corn, are much
smaller, cook faster
and don't need the lid
on the pan. All great
for gluten-free peops!

I got this recipe from my Canadian friend, Juanita,
who has lived in France for a couple of decades. She
mentioned measurements by cups and I replied that we
don't use cups in the UK. It's often more difficult to
be accurate with cups rather than weights. Juanita
doesn't stress about accuracy. "I make some lovely
muffins and I don't measure anything. I just dump it in.
It turns out differently every time but it's edible."
This is her benchmark with food—that it's edible. It's
like Roseanne Barr's attitude to raising children: "As
a housewife, I feel that if the kids are still alive
when my husband gets home from work, then hey, I've
done my job."

So this is a very low-stress, Juanita-style recipe.
Movie-time popcorn, but with the cheesy, healthy flavor
of nutritional yeast. I can't give you the exact amount
of popcorn kernels to use, as it depends on the size
of your receptacle. You want a single layer of popping
corn to cover the base of the pan. Do try to buy as
fresh a corn as you can. I know it's dried, but like
rice, fresher is better. So check those sell-by dates.

■■■■■▪■■■■▪■■✖■■■■■■■■■■■■■■■✦■■■■■▪■■✦◣

Take a large, heavy-bottomed saucepan with a
well-fitting lid. Put in enough oil to cover the
base and add 3 or 4 popping corn kernels. Replace
the lid. Turn the heat up to medium-high. When
those 3 or 4 kernels pop, it's time to add the
rest of the popping corn. Put in enough so that
you have one layer covering the base of the pan.
Replace the lid.

After a few seconds, the popping will commence.
Eventually the sound will subside with only
the odd pop. Take off the heat. Open the lid and
add nutritional yeast flakes and salt to taste.
Pour into a bowl. The best bit is when you've
eaten all the popcorn and you wipe the bottom
of the bowl with your finger, retrieving all the
remaining flavorful remnants.

Roasted Chickpeas

Makes a small jarful

14-oz [400-g] can of
  chickpeas (garbanzo
  beans), drained and
  rinsed

2 Tbsp olive oil

1 tsp ground cumin

1 tsp ground coriander

½ tsp cayenne pepper

1 tsp sea salt

These can be a snack or a topping for soups
and salads. I've also tried this successfully
with soybeans.

Preheat the oven to 325°F [160°C]. Dry the
chickpeas thoroughly using paper towels.
Place on a baking sheet lined with a silicone
baking mat, add the oil, spices, and salt and
thoroughly mix until evenly coated. Spread
them in an even layer and bake for about
1 hour until crisp. Add more seasoning if
you wish. Leave to cool, then store in a dry,
airtight container for up to 2 weeks.

Energy Balls

Makes 15 to 20

10 Medjool dates,
  pitted and finely
  chopped

Scant ½ cup [100 g]
  crunchy peanut
  butter, or other
  nut butter, at room
  temperature

¼ cup [25 g] chopped
  toasted pecans or
  other nuts

1 Tbsp carob molasses

1 Tbsp maple syrup

1 tsp vanilla paste

Pinch of sea salt

To coat:

Toasted coconut

Carob/cocoa powder

Vegan dark chocolate
  sprinkles

Finely ground seeds,
  such as pale green
  pumpkin seeds

Ground pistachio nuts

Poppy seeds

Spirulina powder

Crushed pink
  peppercorns

Beet powder

Ginseng powder

Edible glitter

These little pick-me-ups
are good to keep in your
pocket or bag. Think:
healthy chocolate truffles.
Make the balls, then coat
them in different powders
of your choice, including
edible glitter for party
occasions or gifts.

Blend the dates, nut
butter, and pecans
together in a food
processor, then stir
in the rest of the
ingredients. Set out
small saucers of, say,
3 rolling ingredients
and shape small balls
from the mixture, then
roll them in one of the
coatings, alternating
so that you have a
pretty selection.

Dried Pineapple Flowers

Makes about 10

These are super sweet and pretty. They can be used to decorate cakes or eaten as a snack.

■■■■■■■■■■■■■■■■■■■■■■

1 pineapple

Gold luster dust
(optional)

Preheat the oven to 225°F [110°C].

Top and tail the pineapple by slicing off the top and bottom. Then stand it on a cutting board (tuck a dish towel underneath to stop it wobbling) and, using a sharp knife, carefully remove the skin with a downward motion, turning the pineapple as you work around the sides. Then, with a melon baller or a sharp teaspoon, remove the "eyes" (the brown spiky circles).

Turn the pineapple on its side and slice as thinly as possible: the thinner the slice, the prettier it will look, and the faster it will dry out. Place the slices on a wire rack set over a baking sheet (to enable both sides to dry out).

Bake in the slow oven for 30 to 60 minutes or until they are dry and curling up around the edges. Once they are dried, you could brush the edges with gold luster powder for a pretty effect.

Fruit Leathers

Makes several roll-ups

Like with jam, certain fruits are more suitable than others for fruit leather. For instance, I once tried to make fruit leather from watermelon, which didn't work as well.

Here I used both red and yellow plums. Other fruits that work well include apples, apricots, bananas, berries, cherries, gooseberries (you will need more sugar), mangoes, nectarines, peaches, pears, pineapple, raspberries, and strawberries. Some fruits, such as blueberries, you can use in combination with the more suitable fruits. You could also add small amounts of flavoring, such as juice from freshly minced ginger, ground cinnamon or nutmeg, maple syrup, vanilla extract or paste. You could also add seeds to the leather sheets.

If you have a dehydrator, fruit leather is even easier to make.

2¼ lb [1 kg] plums

4 Tbsp agave nectar

Juice of ½ lemon

I am lucky enough to have a very powerful blender, a Vitamix, which means that I don't have to skin the plums for this recipe. Otherwise, score a cross on the top of each plum with a knife, and leave them for 30 seconds in boiling water. The skin should come off easily. Remove the pits.

Pulse the flesh in a blender, then add the agave nectar and lemon juice. You can use sugar, but an inverted sugar such as agave means that there is less chance of crystallization than with sugar.

Strain the pulp so that there is less juice. For this recipe, I made 2 sheets of "leather"—one that was strained and one that was not. The unstrained leather was more textural and less smooth, but both worked fine. It depends on the fruit. Some fruits have a great deal of juice, so you'd want to strain that out, otherwise you could be drying out the leather for days.

Preheat the oven to 225°F [100°C] and line a flat baking sheet with a silicone baking mat. Using a spatula, spread out the plum purée to about ¼ inch [6 mm] thick. You want it thin enough to dry out, but not so thin that you do not have a "rollable" leather. So make sure you can't see through the purée and remember that it will contract as it dries.

Put in the very slow oven for several hours, checking hourly. If it's not quite dried out when you need to go out or go to bed, turn the oven off after a few hours and leave it (overnight, for example).

When it's sufficiently dried out, carefully peel the leather off the silicone sheet and place it on parchment paper. Cut it into strips and roll it up with strips of the baking parchment. Great for lunchboxes and kids.

Breakfast

A good breakfast sets you
up for the day and means
you are less likely to suffer
from low blood sugar. Here
are a few vegan-friendly
ideas—some are classic, like
muesli or porridge; others
are more exotic, imaginative
replacements for your
boring, routine breakfast.

Drinks

These drink recipes are nutritionally rich and fulfilling, taste-wise. Great for a quick breakfast on the run. You can even make them the night before and keep them in the fridge overnight. A general recipe for nut milk is found on page 29.

For all the recipes below, whizz all the ingredients together, except any garnishes, in a powerful blender such as a Vitamix. (Photo on page 60.)

Mango Lassi

Serves 1

This was a favorite order of mine at Pogo's punk café in London, which held sway for all good animal activists in the noughties. Yes, it was all a bit "Judean People's Front," with many wars between the freegans, the flexitarians and the vegans. Myself—I was accused of not being quite "consensual" enough as a chef in the kitchen, i.e., being a non-PC bossy boots. But some of the food was good.

3 heaping Tbsp [50 ml] mango purée or pulp

3 heaping Tbsp [50 ml] dairy-free coconut yogurt (e.g., CoYo)

Scant ½ cup [100 ml] sweetened soy milk

Seeds of 1 green cardamom pod, ground (¼ tsp)

Handful of ice cubes

Dried mango strips, to garnish

Coconut Smoothie

Serves 1

1 cup [250 ml] coconut milk

Heaping ½ cup [125 ml] dairy-free coconut yogurt (e.g., CoYo)

½ banana, frozen

2 Tbsp agave nectar

Pinch of sea salt

Unsweetened dried coconut shavings, to garnish

Cashew, Banana, & Apricot Smoothie

Serves 2

1 pt [480 ml] Cashew Milk (see page 29)

1 banana, peeled

2 scoops of dairy-free vanilla ice cream (such as Swedish Glace)

5 dried apricots, soaked in cold water for 30 minutes, then drained

2 Tbsp agave nectar

1 tsp vanilla paste

Mexican Chocolate Shake

Serves 2

A little spice to get you going in the morning. Dark chocolate lowers blood pressure and alleviates depression. Cocoa nibs are like amphetamines for the clean living.

1½ cups [360 ml] oat, almond, or hazelnut milk

1 oz [30 g] vegan dark chocolate

1 Tbsp cocoa nibs (optional)

1 to 2 Tbsp cocoa powder, plus extra to garnish

½ tsp ground cinnamon

2 Tbsp agave nectar

½ tsp chipotle paste (optional)

Handful of ice cubes

Mean, Lean, & Green Shake

Serves 2

Green juice is all the rage amongst dieters and health freaks. Now that the current advice is to eat "7 a day" (5 vegetables and 2 fruits), you can bust through about half of that in this one green smoothie.

⅔ cup [100 g] seedless green grapes

2 cups [100 g] baby spinach, any big stems removed

½ cucumber, peeled

½ avocado, peeled and pitted

¾ cup [100 g] blueberries, plus extra to garnish

A few sprigs of parsley

Large pinch of alfalfa sprouts

Juice of ½ lemon

1 scant cup [200 ml] water

1 tsp spirulina powder (optional)

Light-as-Air Crumpets

Makes 16

Dare I say it, but these are even lighter and more delicious than standard English crumpets. Slather with tahini, agave nectar, Marmite, or jam.

....

½ cup [70 g] white bread flour

½ cup + ½ Tbsp [70 g] all-purpose flour

2¼ tsp [¼-oz/7-g envelope] active dry yeast

½ tsp sea salt

1 tsp superfine sugar

1⅛ cups [275 ml] warm almond milk

¼ tsp baking soda

Scant ½ cup [100 ml] warm water

Melted coconut oil, for greasing and cooking

Equipment:

Cast-iron or good-quality heavy-bottomed skillet or griddle

At least 4 metal crumpet or egg rings or plain metal pastry cutters, about 3 in [7.5 cm] diameter

Heatproof pastry brush

Mix together the flours, yeast, and salt in a bowl. Add the sugar and warm almond milk and beat together until you have a smooth batter. Cover and leave to rise in a warm place for 45 minutes.

Mix the baking soda into the water, then leave for a couple of minutes before adding it to the batter. Cover again and leave to rest for 20 minutes.

Heat your skillet (or griddle) over medium-high heat. You want it quite hot, but not so hot that the crumpets burn on the outside before they are cooked on the inside. Arrange a little pot of melted coconut oil, the pastry brush and the batter with a small ladle or tablespoon next to the stovetop.

You'll need to cook your crumpets in batches. Add a little oil to the pan and grease the insides of the metal rings (or cutters) using the pastry brush. Allow the rings to heat up in the pan and then, using the small ladle (or tablespoon), fill each ring to a depth of no more than ¾ in [2 cm]. (Don't overfill them or they will take too long to cook and the holes won't have enough time to form).

Now wait. Be patient. Only turn your crumpets over once the surface is set and lots of holes have appeared through the top of the batter. Then, using tongs or the corner of a dish towel, lift away the rings, flip over the crumpets using a spatula and continue cooking briefly for a minute or so on the other side. This way you can get a rolling system going, using the empty hot metal rings for the next batch, greasing them with oil as you go (be careful, as the rings will be hot!) and ladling in more batter, while the first batch, having set their shape in the rings, continues to cook. Cook the remaining crumpets in the same way until they are all done.

Transfer the cooked crumpets to a wire rack. To keep them hot, lay them one by one in a large "envelope" of foil and keep them in the oven on its lowest setting.

Black Cat Pancakes with Bananas, Cinnamon, & Maple Syrup

Makes about 8

Carolyn Stapleton is the chef of a vegan restaurant near "murder mile" in Clapton called the Black Cat on the site of the old Pogo café. She's a fantastic cook!

Here is her recipe for fluffy vegan pancakes.

½ banana, peeled

¼ cup [50 g] superfine sugar

1 cup [250 ml] soy or other dairy-free milk

1¾ cups + 2 Tbsp [250 g] self-rising flour

1 level Tbsp baking powder

Pinch of sea salt

3 heaping Tbsp [50 ml] sparkling water

1 tsp coconut oil (optional)

To serve:

1 to 2 bananas, peeled and sliced

1 tsp ground cinnamon

Maple syrup

Coconut oil or vegan spread

In a food processor, blend the banana, sugar, and half the milk together, then transfer to a stand mixer or a bowl.

Whisk in the flour and remaining milk, then add the baking powder, salt, and sparkling water. (I have used sparkling elderflower drink when I didn't have any sparkling water, and this worked fine too!) The thicker the mixture, the thicker and more pillowy your pancakes will be, so aim for a consistency that is just about pourable, something like heavy cream.

To cook, heat up a flat skillet or "crêpière." You can cook them in a dry pan or just rub it slightly with a little coconut oil. Using a large spoon, ladle in about 2 spoonfuls per pancake. Wait until bubbles start to form before flipping them over. When both sides are golden and pillowy, transfer to a heatproof plate, cover with foil and keep warm in the oven on its lowest setting.

Cook the remaining pancakes in the same way until they are all done. Serve with the sliced banana, cinnamon, maple syrup and coconut oil or vegan spread.

Chirpy Muesli

Makes 3¼ lb [1.5 kg]

½ cup [125 ml] nut oil, such as almond or hazelnut

⅔ cup [150 ml] maple syrup or agave nectar

1 tsp vanilla extract

18 oz [500 g] rolled oats

½ cup [50 g] pecans, roughly chopped

Scant 1¼ cups [150 g] hazelnuts, roughly chopped

½ cup [75 g] pumpkin seeds

½ cup [75 g] sunflower seeds

⅜ cup [50 g] golden linseed (flaxseed)

1⅓ cups [100 g] dried, grated coconut

10½ oz [300 g] mixed dried fruit, such as dates, figs, apricots, raisins, golden raisins, cranberries, mulberries, sour cherries, blueberries (the larger fruit should be chopped)

To serve:

Soy, rice, oat, or nut milk

Fresh fruit, such as sliced bananas

Here is a good recipe for muesli without honey. Feel free to change the nuts and fruit to whatever you happen to have in your pantry. There are so many seeds and nuts in it (unlike the forlorn culinary treasure hunt you have to do with storebought) that you might end up chirping cheerfully like a bird throughout the morning. I served this at a pop-up restaurant I ran at Bestival music festival and people came up to me saying it was without a doubt the best muesli they'd ever eaten. This will last up to 2 months in a dry place.

Preheat the oven to 325°F [160°C].

Put the oil, maple syrup or agave nectar, and vanilla extract in a small saucepan over low heat and gently melt together.

Mix the oats, nuts, seeds, and coconut together in a large bowl. Pour over the melted oil mixture and stir really well to ensure all the dry ingredients are evenly coated.

Divide the mixture between 2 large baking sheets and spread it out in an even layer. Bake in the oven for 20 to 25 minutes, tossing every 5 minutes, until golden brown. Remove from the oven and leave to cool on the sheets, stirring every now and then. (If you transfer it to a deep bowl while still warm, it will go soggy.)

Once completely cool, transfer to a large bowl and stir in your choice of dried fruits. Serve with the dairy-free milk of your choice and top with fresh fruit.

Porridge with Rhubarb, Date Sugar, & Cardamom Compote

Serves 1

Porridge (oatmeal) has so many health benefits that I hardly need mention them. One of the most rewarding aspects of porridge is that you will not feel hungry for at least 4 to 5 hours after eating it, due to the slow release of complex carbohydrate energy. There are many different toppings for porridge, and this is only one suggestion. If rhubarb is not in season, then simply slice up a few apples and sprinkle with ground cinnamon. Cinnamon is nature's blood sugar regulator.

I love rhubarb, both the tender, crimson forced stems in winter, and the thicker, rougher stuff you get in spring (from which you should remove any particularly stringy spines). It is a vegetable, and buckwheat is related to it. Don't eat the leaves, as they are toxic, but keep the leaves on until you are ready to use it.

For the compote:

3 rhubarb stalks, trimmed and cut into 2 in [5 cm] batons

3 Tbsp date sugar (or coconut palm or cane sugar), or to taste

3 green cardamom pods, crushed

For the porridge:

⅓ cup [50 g] organic medium oats (Scottish oatmeal)

1¼ cups [300 ml] oat milk, e.g., Pacific Natural Foods (you can use water or soy milk, but I found oat milk perfectly complements porridge, being made of oats)

Large pinch of sea salt

To make the compote, preheat the oven to 400°F [200°C]. Mix the rhubarb, sugar, and cardamom in a baking dish, cover with foil, and bake for 10 to 15 minutes. Add more sugar to taste, if necessary.

You could soak the oatmeal overnight in the milk, as this does make a softer gruel. Otherwise, put the oats and the milk into a medium saucepan over medium-high heat and bring to a boil while stirring. Once the porridge starts to bubble, turn down the heat and simmer for 10 minutes. About 5 minutes before the end, add the salt and keep stirring. Top with the compote, eat, and feel satisfied.

Scrambled Tofu on Truffled Sourdough Bruschetta

Serves 4

3 to 4 Tbsp olive oil

2 scallions, finely sliced

6 to 8 medium brown
mushrooms, sliced

7 oz [200 g] silken tofu,
drained and crumbled

1 Tbsp thyme, oregano, or
marjoram leaves

4 slices of sourdough or
other good bread

1 garlic clove, halved

Truffle oil or truffle paste

Handful of basil leaves,
shredded

Sea salt and freshly ground
black pepper

This is vaguely like scrambled eggs, but not really. It's a very easy, quick breakfast and can be flavored any which way: Mexican, Indian, Italian. The truffle turns it into a bit of a luxury. Tofu is a great flavor absorber. For this scramble, use firm, but silken tofu and drain it. This is one of my favorite dishes in the book—absolutely delicious.

Heat the oil in a skillet over medium heat, and when hot, sprinkle in the scallions, mushrooms, tofu, and herbs. With a spatula, fry the tofu until it looks dry, like scrambled eggs. Season with salt and pepper to taste.

In the meantime, toast the bread, then rub with the cut garlic clove. Drizzle over the truffle oil or paste.

Serve both together, with the shredded basil as a garnish, and if you like, a couple of turns of fresh black pepper from the mill.

Tofu Shakshouka

Serves 2

Good slug of olive oil

Half a dozen cherry
tomatoes, cut in half

1 red bell pepper, seeded,
and cut into thin strips

5 scallions, preferably
purple, chopped into
rounds, plus extra, sliced
lengthwise, to garnish

5 garlic cloves, cut into
slivers

14-oz [400-g] can of chopped
tomatoes

1 Tbsp sweet paprika

1 Tbsp freshly ground
coriander seeds

1 tsp ground cumin

A few saffron strands

1 tsp dried red pepper
flakes, or more, to taste

Sea salt, to taste

Scoop of soy yogurt,
to serve (optional)

14 oz [400 g] silken tofu,
drained, and cut into
cubes (on your palm—see
recipe introduction, page
106—or in the box)

Warm pita bread, to serve

I visited Israel in 2012 and the food is downright amazing. These people like to eat and know what to eat. One of the most popular breakfasts is shakshouka, which is a dish of eggs cooked in a spicy red tomato sauce. I visited a vegetarian/vegan restaurant there called Ornella and Ella, and I had the tofu shakshouka. I was supposed to share it with my companion, but it was so delicious that I scoffed it all in one sitting. I'm a big fan of tofu for taking on flavors so willingly. Silken tofu provides a delightful textural contrast here.

Heat the oil in a good-quality skillet, ideally nonstick. Then add the cherry tomatoes and the red bell pepper strips and fry until slightly golden. Add the scallions. Ditto.

Add the garlic, tomatoes, paprika, ground coriander, cumin, saffron, red pepper flakes, and salt. Stir briefly to combine. Now add the tofu, but don't stir, otherwise you might break it up—it's delicate. Leave to cook over medium-high heat for 20 to 30 minutes until all the tomatoes seem cooked through, and the tofu has sort of poached into a silky wobbliness, but still retains a cube-like shape. Add some more water or tomato liquid if the mixture becomes too dry.

Add a scoop of soy yogurt, if you like, and some purple scallions on top. Eat with warm pita bread. Really, this is a dish to convince non-veggies.

Quesadillas with Black Beans & Tofu, Huitlacoche, & Rajas

Serves 4

I used to live in Los Angeles, where I worked in a photographic lab printing pictures by famous photographers. Every morning a Mexican food truck would pull up at about 11 A.M. and I'd order a cheesy green chile quesadilla. Heaven! At that time I was going to the gym every day doing Jane Fonda-style "aerobics"—remember them?—so I could afford to eat my body weight in fat 'n' carbs. This is a vegan version, equally tasty but rather healthier. Huitlacoche is a fungus that grows on corn, which I'll admit sounds disgusting, but absolutely isn't. (What do you think mushrooms are?) Rajas are tinned strips of poblano chile, which are very mild but tasty. You can buy huitlacoche and rajas online at Mexican food sites (like www.mexgrocer.com and www.mymexicanpantry.com). They are the authentic taste of Mexican cooking. If you need that cheesy feel, then use one of the stretchier vegan cheeses such as Daiya, sold in slices. You could also add slices of avocado and soy yogurt as "sour" cream.

This is a great recipe for a weekend brunch to share with family or friends. I've got a few ingredients here, so you could lay them all out and mix and match.

Olive oil, for frying

1 onion, diced

1 red bell pepper, seeded and thinly sliced

1 jalapeño chile, seeded and chopped

1 Tbsp chopped garlic

14-oz [400-g] can of black beans (or pinto beans if unavailable), drained

1 qt [1 L] vegetable stock

Juice of 1 lime

3 tsp ground cumin

1¾ oz [50 g] vegan dark chocolate (optional)

1 chipotle, roasted and then soaked (see page 19)

1 Tbsp sweet paprika, plus 1 tsp

1 Tbsp fresh or dried thyme leaves

Large handful of chopped cilantro leaves

A few drops of chipotle or Tabasco sauce

14 oz [400 g] firm tofu, drained and sliced ⅜ in [1 cm] thick

1 small can of huitlacoche (or mushrooms), drained

Handful of green rajas (or mild green chiles/jalapeños, roasted, seeded, skinned, and cut into strips) from a small can, plus extra to serve

16 small or 8 large wheat tortillas

Vegan melty cheese, sliced (optional)

Sea salt and freshly ground black pepper

To serve:

Avocado slices

Soy yogurt

Lime wedges

Cilantro leaves

To make the black bean chili, heat 2 Tbsp olive oil in a saucepan over medium heat and fry the onion until soft, then season with salt and pepper. Add the red bell pepper, jalapeño, garlic, and beans. Continue to fry for a couple of minutes, then add the stock and lime juice. Add 2 tsp cumin, chocolate, if using, chipotle, 1 Tbsp paprika and thyme leaves. Lower the heat and cook for 30 minutes. Check the seasoning, then remove from the heat, stir in the cilantro and set aside in a bowl.

Heat some olive oil in a skillet, then add the 1 tsp paprika, 1 tsp cumin, 1 tsp salt and chipotle or Tabasco sauce. Add the tofu and fry lightly until warmed through. Add the huitlacoche (or mushrooms) and a few of the rajas (or green chile) strips, stirring carefully so as not to break up the tofu. Set aside in a bowl.

You will need to cook these in batches, 1 to 2 at a time depending on the size of the tortillas and your skillet. Lay out 2 tortillas and spread the black bean chili in a thin layer, then the tofu mixture. If you have vegan cheese, add that in slices too. Place 2 tortillas, over the top, pressing down slightly.

Fry the assembled tortillas in a dry, flat skillet over medium heat, flipping them over once the underneath tortilla starts to brown. Once the other side is done, remove from the heat and cut into quarters. Keep hot in a slow oven while you repeat with the remaining tortillas until they're all done.

Serve with avocado slices, soy yogurt, some more of the rajas, lime wedges, and cilantro leaves.

Poppy Seed Waffles with Blueberries, Orange Zest, & Maple Syrup

Makes 4 to 8

Vegan butter or coconut oil,
    for greasing

For the waffles:

¼ cup [50 g] superfine sugar

1½ tsp baking powder

Heaping 1¾ cups [250 g]
    all-purpose flour

1 cup [250 ml] hemp or rice
    milk

⅓ cup [75 g] coconut oil,
    melted

1 tsp vanilla paste

2 Tbsp poppy seeds

For the blueberry sauce:

1⅛ cups [150 g] blueberries

¼ cup [50 g] sugar

3 Tbsp maple syrup, plus
    extra to serve

Zest and juice of
    1 orange

Equipment:

Waffle maker

I love poppy seeds; they are basically drugs; a mild form of opium. Remember that episode in *Seinfeld* where Julia Louis-Dreyfus tests positive for heroin? Turns out she was eating too many poppy-seed bagels. So it goes without saying that this is a feel-good recipe, perfect for a weekend breakfast. Trippy.

Heat up your waffle maker and grease with vegan butter or coconut oil.

Mix the waffle ingredients together in a bowl.

Put the blueberries, sugar, maple syrup, and orange zest and juice in a medium saucepan over medium-high heat, keeping back a little of the orange zest to serve. Stir until the blueberries start to break down but have not lost their shape entirely. Then take off the heat and set aside.

Ladle just enough of the waffle batter to fill the waffle maker sections, then spread it around. Close the lid and cook for 3 to 5 minutes, or according to the manufacturer's instructions. Transfer to a heatproof plate, cover with foil, and keep warm in the oven on its lowest setting.

Cook the remaining waffles in the same way until they are all done. Serve the waffles hot with the blueberry sauce, a little extra maple syrup, and the reserved orange zest.

Lunch

These light dishes are
perfect for lunch. But if
you are throwing a formal
dinner party, you could
make some of these recipes
as starters and follow them
with something from the
Dinner chapter.

Soy Soup with Silken Tofu & Edamame Beans

Serves 4

Scant 3 cups [700 ml]
   unsweetened soy milk

4-in [10-cm] piece of kombu

1 heaping Tbsp white miso

2 tsp yuzu paste

2 tsp light soy sauce

14-oz [400-g] block of
   silken tofu, drained

⅔ cup [75 g] edamame beans,
   podded

Sea salt

Japanese nanami togarashi
   (chili seasoning),
   to garnish

A subtle, refreshing and delicate soup.
Very clean and fresh tasting.

In a medium saucepan over very low heat, gently warm the soy milk with the piece of kombu, then take it off the heat and leave to infuse for about 30 minutes.

Return the pan to the heat and add the miso, yuzu paste, and soy sauce. Cut the block of tofu into quarters, then cut each quarter in half crosswise. Add the slices to the soup and poach them over low heat for 5 to 10 minutes. Finally, add the edamame beans, reserving a handful to serve. Season with salt to taste.

Ladle the soup into 4 bowls, with 2 slices of silken tofu in the middle. Fish out the piece of kombu and discard. Sprinkle a few edamame beans on top of the soup, and sprinkle with the nanami togarashi.

Zurek Sour Rye Soup

Serves 4 to 6

Homemade sour rye liquid:

Scant ⅓ cup [40 g] dark
  rye flour

1 qt [1 L] warm water

2 fresh bay leaves

2 allspice berries

2 garlic cloves, sliced

For the soup:

1 cup [20 g] dried porcini
  mushrooms

1 cup [250 ml] boiling
  water

5 Tbsp [75 ml] olive oil

5 shallots, sliced

4 garlic cloves, sliced

Scant 1¾ lb [750 g] waxy
  potatoes, peeled and cut
  into small cubes

6 in [15 cm] celery stalk,
  thinly sliced

2 fresh bay leaves

3 allspice berries

1 tsp marjoram or oregano
  leaves

A few sprigs of thyme

5 black or green
  peppercorns

1 qt [1 L] sour rye
  liquid, strained (see
  above)

A few shavings of fresh
  horseradish

Sea salt and white pepper

For the garnish:

Fresh porcini, shiitake, or
  button mushrooms, sliced

1 garlic clove

Handful of dill, minced

Sour soups in Eastern Europe are made using
fermented rye (or wheat). This is one you
have to start 2 days in advance in order
to ferment the rye flour, but you can buy
the sour liquid known as "zakwas," a liquid
sourdough starter, in Polish and Eastern
European food shops. Anything fermented is
healthy for the flora and fauna of your gut.

Homemade sour rye liquid:

Put the flour, water, bay leaves, and
allspice berries in a jar and cover the
jar with cheesecloth (it needs access
to the air to ferment). Leave in a warm
place for 2 days, stirring carefully twice
a day. After 2 days, add the garlic. If
any sediment forms on the top—which is
harmless—scrape it off. Once fermented (it
should look a bit bubbly and smell slightly
sour), strain it and reserve the liquid.

For the soup:

Rinse the dried porcini of dust, put into
a small bowl, pour over the boiling water
and set aside to soak.

Heat 3 Tbsp [50 ml] of the olive oil in
a large, heavy-bottomed saucepan, add the
shallots, and fry until soft, then add
the garlic, potatoes, celery, bay leaves,
allspice berries, marjoram or oregano,
thyme, peppercorns, and 1 Tbsp salt. Fry
for a few minutes until the potatoes start
to color, then add the sour liquid and the
soaked porcini with their soaking liquid.

Bring to a boil, then turn down the heat
and simmer for 15 to 20 minutes until the
potatoes are tender and the mushrooms are
soft. Check the seasoning, adding salt
if needed, and white pepper to taste. If
you'd like the soup more liquid, you could
add 2 cups [480 ml] vegetable or mushroom
stock at this stage. Grate in some fresh
horseradish and cook for another 20 minutes
or so. Remove the bay leaves if you wish.
Fry up the fresh mushrooms for the garnish
with the garlic in the remaining 2 Tbsp
olive oil, then serve the soup topped with
the fried mushrooms and dill.

Hot & Sour Soup

Serves 6

3 to 4 Tbsp peanut or vegetable oil

3 garlic cloves, minced

1-in [2.5-cm] piece of ginger, peeled and grated (I keep mine in the freezer to use as and when)

5¼ oz (150 g) shiitake mushrooms, sliced

5 to 7 oz (150 to 200 g) brown mushrooms, sliced

2 red chiles, seeded and thinly sliced

Big glug of rice wine or dry sherry

2 qt [2 L] hot vegetable stock

4 lime leaves (ideally fresh: grow a kaffir lime plant to always have some around)

Scant 3 Tbsp [40 ml] light soy sauce

Scant 2 Tbsp [25 ml] dark soy sauce

Scant ¼ cup [50 ml] Chinese black vinegar

Juice of 4 limes

3 Tbsp cornstarch mixed with 6 Tbsp cold water, OR 9 oz [250 g] ramen noodles

1 cup [100 g] baby corn cobs, halved lengthwise

1 heaping cup [100 g] snow peas

A few carrots, finely julienned (optional)

5 oz [150 g] silken tofu, drained and cut into ⅝-inch [1.5-cm] cubes (see page 106)

For the garnish:

1 bunch of scallions, julienned

Handful of bean sprouts, well washed

Mint and cilantro leaves

I served this at The Secret Garden Club supper club that I host monthly with gardener Zia Mays. We try to use the produce that I grow in my garden. This time the theme was herbs—classic, unusual and micro. This hot and sour soup is a bit of a mix between a Thai sour soup and a Chinese one. I found that just the black vinegar wasn't sour enough, so I added lime. A proper Chinese hot and sour soup has wood ears and bamboo shoots in it. I didn't have any, so this is my bastardized version. Fear not, it was damn good even if not entirely authentic.

It's also very Chinese if all the vegetables are julienned (cut into fine strips) and the tofu precisely cut into squares.

Heat the oil in a large pan and add the garlic, ginger, and both types of mushroom. Fry for 5 to 10 minutes until the mushrooms are golden, then add the chiles and rice wine or sherry. Stir for a couple of minutes.

Add the stock, lime leaves, soy sauces, vinegar, and lime juice. Taste for the required balance of heat (chile), sour (lime and vinegar) and salt (soy sauces). Adjust the balance as needed.

Add the cornstarch paste (unless you will be adding noodles later; don't add both or it will be too starchy) and simmer for 30 minutes. Next add the baby corn, snow peas, carrots if using, and tofu, with the noodles if you haven't added cornstarch.

Simmer for 5 minutes, or longer to cook the noodles, then ladle into bowls and top with the scallions and bean sprouts, then the herbs.

Sweet Potato & Coconut South Seas Soup

Serves 4

3 to 5 Tbsp [50 to 75 ml]
vegetable or palm oil

1 red onion, diced

4 garlic cloves, minced

1 red chile, seeded and
very finely chopped

2-in [5 cm] piece of
ginger, peeled and very
finely chopped

1 tsp toasted coriander
seeds, freshly ground

1 tsp ground turmeric

Pinch of saffron strands

2 sticks of lemongrass,
very thinly sliced

1 red bell pepper, seeded
and cut into strips

1 large sweet potato,
peeled and cut into
1½-in [4-cm] cubes

3⅓ cups [400 ml] coconut
milk

Juice of 1 lime, plus
extra to serve

2 cups [100 g] spinach

Sea salt

Cilantro leaves,
to serve

I made a scaled-up version of this soup at music festival Bestival when I did a desert island/pirate/18th-century shipboard-inspired pop-up. We had a sea-shanty band, rigging in the tent, napkins made from map fabric ("mapkins"), maps as menus, vintage globes, and costumes created especially for the crew. Bawdy singing and rum were the order of the day.

I have to admit, cooking in a field is a challenge. For a start, at festivals, none of the staff want to work much. They want to be out there, having fun with everyone else. Oh, I give long, stern lectures beforehand about how they are getting paid and they must be professional. This lecture never works. Luckily, this is a simple soup to make, so I managed to serve it to 800 people without TOO much sweat.

Heat the oil in a large saucepan over medium heat, add the onion and cook until softened, then add the garlic, chile, ginger, ground coriander, turmeric, saffron, lemongrass, and 1 Tbsp sea salt. Stir well, then add the red bell pepper and sweet potato and fry until lightly golden around the edges.

Add the coconut milk and lime juice and simmer for 10 to 15 minutes, adding the spinach just before the end; it will wilt in the heat of the soup. Season to taste with salt.

Ladle into bowls, add more lime juice and the cilantro and serve with the sambal below.

Coconut, Lime, & Chile Sambal

Serves 4 as a garnish for the soup

1 fresh coconut

2 fresh red chiles,
seeded and very finely
chopped

Juice of 2 limes

Handful of cilantro
leaves

Sea salt

Open the coconut (see page 18), draining the milk into a glass. Peel off the brown skin. Put the milk and flesh in a Vitamix or powerful food processor. Add the chiles, lime juice, cilantro, and salt to taste, and process until finely minced.

Tortilla & Squash Blossom Soup

Serves 4 to 6

This is a big favorite in the United States and Mexico, but you don't see it very much in the UK. Do not be afraid: the high proportion of dried chilies is not spicy, as pasilla and anchos are very mild. They do give a deep, authentic taste to the soup. This is a very Frida Kahlo-esque soup—colorful and floral. I once did a Frida Kahlo-themed supper club and almost every guest arrived with a drawn-on monobrow.

Only add the flowers toward the end of the cooking, as they just need to wilt in the steam of the soup. But if they are the female zucchini flowers, which have a tiny zucchini attached, cook them a little longer in the heat of the soup so that the zucchini part softens a bit.

You can use zucchini flowers or any flowers from squash, but remove the larger stamens from squash flowers. Check the insides for insects. To obtain these flowers, make friends with a gardener, or ideally, grow your own.

5 dried pasilla or ancho chilies

3 to 5 garlic cloves, unpeeled

Olive or vegetable oil

2 white onions, diced

5 tomatoes, diced

3 cups [750 ml] vegetable stock

⅜ to ¾ in [1 to 2 cm] achiote paste (available from Mexican online shops)

10 to 15 squash or zucchini flowers

Juice of 1 lime

Handful of cilantro leaves

Sea salt

4 to 6 corn tortillas, cut into strips and fried, OR blue or white corn tortilla chips, to garnish

Soak the chilies as described on page 19, retaining the red-colored soaking water.

In the meantime, toast the garlic cloves in a little oil in a skillet over low heat until softened—about 15 minutes. Slip off the skins and blend the garlic in a food processor with the drained chilies and a little of the reserved red chili water.

Fry the onions in some oil in a large saucepan until soft, then add the tomatoes and fry lightly. Add the chili and garlic mixture and stir well. Then add the stock and achiote paste, taste and add a little salt, depending on how salty your stock is.

Cook for at least 30 minutes over medium-low heat, stirring from time to time, then add the squash or zucchini flowers and lime juice. Check and adjust the seasoning and add the cilantro leaves.

Ladle the soup into bowls, top with the fried tortilla strips or chips and serve immediately.

Smoky Salmorejo with Basil Oil

Serves 4

8 ripe smoked tomatoes, quartered (or add a few drops of liquid smoke to fresh tomatoes)

2 garlic cloves, peeled

1 baguette (about 9 oz [250 g]), sliced

½ onion

Scant 1 cup [200 ml] extra-virgin olive oil

2 Tbsp sherry vinegar

1 Tbsp smoked paprika

5 cups [125 g] fresh basil leaves, blended with 3 Tbsp olive oil

Sea salt and freshly ground black pepper

This is the Madrileño version of the Andalucian gazpacho. If you're confident at cold smoking, you can make your own smoked tomatoes by halving and dehydrating 8 ripe tomatoes in a very slow oven for 4 to 6 hours before cold smoking them.

Place 3 Tbsp sea salt (or 3 tsp table salt), the tomatoes, garlic, bread, and onion in a large bowl and cover with boiling water. Leave for 45 minutes, then drain out the water, squeezing the bread, and keeping back 1 cup for blending purposes.

Place the drained vegetables and bread in a blender or food processor with the reserved liquid and add the oil, vinegar, and smoked paprika. Purée until smooth, then check the seasoning, adding pepper and more salt if necessary. Chill in the fridge—overnight if possible, to allow the flavors to meld.

Serve chilled and garnished with the basil oil alongside a cool glass of dry sherry.

Ajo Blanco with Pickled Green Pepper Relish

Serves 4

For the green pepper relish:

2 green bell peppers

Olive oil

5 Tbsp [75 ml] white wine vinegar

2 Tbsp granulated sugar

2 Tbsp sea salt

1 tsp drained pickled green peppercorns

1 Tbsp drained baby capers

Handful of flat-leaf parsley leaves, to garnish

For the soup:

1 heaping cup [150 g] blanched almonds

6 garlic cloves, peeled

2 cups [100 g] fresh sourdough bread crumbs

2 cups [480 ml] cold water

2 tsp sea salt

Scant 1 cup [200 ml] extra-virgin olive oil

2 to 3 Tbsp white balsamic or sherry vinegar, to taste

White pepper

A chilled Spanish soup made from almonds and garlic. Simple and pale, but elegantly filling. You'll only need a small portion.

Preheat the oven to 400°F [200°C]. To make the green pepper relish, place the green bell peppers on a baking sheet, toss in a little olive oil and roast in the oven for 15 to 20 minutes until the skin is blackened. Place in a plastic bag for 5 minutes, then strip off the shiny skin and seed them.

In a small saucepan, combine the wine vinegar, sugar, and salt and place over medium heat until the sugar and salt have dissolved. Remove from the heat and let cool completely.

Tear or slice the peppers into strips and add to the cooled pickling liquid with the peppercorns and capers. Then heat until the vinegar evaporates.

For the soup, briefly toast the almonds in a dry skillet over medium-high heat for no more than 1 to 2 minutes. Transfer to a plate and leave to cool, then process in a blender with the garlic, bread crumbs, water, salt, olive oil, and balsamic or sherry vinegar. Chill in the fridge until ready to serve.

Season the chilled soup with white pepper, then ladle into bowls, place a little green pepper relish in the middle of each and scatter over a few parsley leaves.

Popcorn Chowder with Achiote

Serves 4

I developed this chunky fresh soup for another Bestival menu. People from all
over Britain go to this music festival, but pass rapidly through the picture-
perfect countryside, which is a shame because the Isle of Wight has some of the
best ingredients in Britain. With this recipe I was attempting to bring the Isle of
Wight back into the festival by using local seasonal ingredients. I got this corn
from farmer Ben Brown from Arreton, just a mile down the road from the festival.
The corn was so sweet you could eat it raw, straight from the cob, like sugar.

I served this in soup bowl-sized pumpkins, again from Ben Brown, oiled, salted and
lightly roasted prior to filling them with soup.

4 little pumpkins,
the size of bowls

Corn or vegetable oil

2 fresh corn cobs

1 small onion, diced

1 garlic clove, minced

¾ inch [2 cm] achiote
paste (available
from Mexican
websites)

1 to 2 whole chipotle
chilies in adobo
sauce (depending
on your heat
tolerance), finely
diced

3 Tbsp cornmeal or
masa harina (NOT
cornstarch)

Scant 1 pt [450 ml]
hot vegetable stock

1¼ cups [300 ml] soy
cream

1 tsp sweet smoked
paprika, plus extra
to garnish

Sea salt

For the garnish:

½ cup [100 g] popping
corn

A little corn oil

Handful of cilantro
leaves, to garnish

Preheat the oven to 400°F [200°C].

First prepare the pumpkins. Slice off the top
(which will be the lid), then hollow out the
center, leaving enough flesh inside the skin
so that the soup will not leak. Discard the
insides. Oil the outside of the pumpkin bowls
and lids, rub sea salt inside and out and
roast for 15–20 minutes. Leave to cool.

Grasp each corn cob firmly upright on a board
and slice downwards on each side using a
sharp knife; the kernels should fall away
quite easily.

Sweat the onion in a large pan in some oil,
then add the garlic, achiote paste, and corn.
Lightly sauté, then add the chipotle and stir
well. Add the cornmeal or masa harina, hot
stock, soy cream, 2 tsp salt, and the smoked
paprika. Check and adjust the seasoning.

Bring to a boil, then simmer for at least
20 minutes. This soup does deepen in flavor if
you keep it going. I mention a minimum here,
but I often feel soup is better the next day.

Meanwhile, put the popping corn and a little
corn oil in a large saucepan with a well-
fitting lid and place over high heat. Once the
popping subsides, leave behind the unpopped
kernels and season the rest with sea salt and
the sweet smoked paprika.

Ladle the hot soup into the pumpkin bowls,
top with a few cilantro leaves and some
popcorn and serve.

Peruvian Purple Potato
Papa a la Huancaína

Serves 4

I spent three months in Peru, one of the world's most interesting countries. Unlike most tourists, I spent some time up in the north, at a place called Kuelap, a first-century ruined city at the top of a remote hillside. Rumor has it that tall white people inhabited it, possibly Vikings. This is way before the Spanish arrived and hundreds of years before the Incas.

This Peruvian dish is from a little-visited inland town, Huancayo, to which you can take a train from Lima. It's one of the highest-altitude train rides, almost 16,000 ft [5,000 m] in places, in the world. When I embarked upon this journey, 25 years ago, it looked like a bus or tram on a very narrow train track. The back of the carriage was stored with oxygen tankards in case people could not cope with the thin air.

Ideally, this classic recipe uses yellow chilies (aji amarillo), but they aren't easy to get hold of. There is an online resource (www. amigofoods.com), but you can substitute with any fruity, pale chili sauce.

Use the best potatoes you can buy: most impressively, purple potatoes such as Purple Majesty by Albert Bartlett, or rich, waxy yellow Yukon Gold potatoes, or a mixture of both.

4 large purple potatoes, unpeeled

1 tsp aji amarillo paste (see introduction)

1 garlic clove, minced

1 cup [250 ml] soy cream

2 Tbsp nutritional yeast

Juice of ½ lime

Sea salt

To garnish:

Lime wedges

Sprigs of cilantro

Put the potatoes into a large saucepan, cover with boiling water, add 1 Tbsp salt, and cook over high heat. Purple potatoes cook a lot more quickly than white, in maybe half the time, so keep an eye on them. Once the potatoes are cooked, drain and leave to cool. Then slip off the skins and cut into ⅝-inch [1.5-cm] slices.

Meanwhile, put the aji amarillo paste, garlic, soy cream, nutritional yeast, lime juice, and 1 tsp salt into a blender and process until smooth. Pour into a small saucepan and heat until warmed through and slightly thickened.

To plate up: first pour the sauce onto the plate, then add the purple potato slices. Garnish with lime wedges and cilantro and serve.

Salmagundi

This is a tall layered salad, popular in the 18th century. Hannah Glasse mentions it in her 1747 book, *The Art of Cookery Made Plain and Easy*. I served it at a Soil Association pop-up in Toynbee Hall in London's Tower Hamlets, in a wood-paneled banqueting room. This is not a strict recipe as such; more a compilation of things you can put in it. It's spectacular when done right. If you have a garden, add stalks of herb flowers and edible flowers to turn it into an extravagant display. Who says vegan food is dowdy? Not done like this it isn't. Serve it with dips from the Snacks chapter.

You want height on this dish; you could do individual portions in tea cups, then invert them, or use a bowl or a ring mold for cake. Or just construct it gradually, like a piece of architecture, shaping the vegetables to fit, inserting sprigs as you go, alternating colors and textures. Or you can pop the dips in little cut-glass bowls on a large silver tray, stuffing the surroundings with a burgeoning garden-like salad. This is an eye-popping, wow-inducing centerpiece like a fresh savory croquembouche.

Romaine lettuce leaves

Red and white Belgian endive

Arugula

Watercress

Fennel, thinly sliced, keeping the fronds on

Sorrel leaves

Cucumber slices

Tomatoes, carved like flowers or roses if you have the time

Carrot batons

Red bell pepper batons

Cauliflower florets

Broccoli florets

Wild asparagus stems

Sage leaves, both plain and variegated

Cornflowers

Nasturtiums

Lavender sprigs

Pea shoots

Chive lengths, if possible with purple flowers if in season

Parsley stalks, curly

Red radishes, decoratively cut

Shallots, finely diced

Strawberries

Hazelnuts

Green olives stuffed with pimentos or lemon

Borage flowers

Dill fronds

Pumpkin seeds

For the classic Dijon mustard dressing:

3½ Tbsp [50 ml] extra-virgin olive oil

1 heaping Tbsp Dijon mustard

1 garlic clove, minced

Juice of ½ lemon

1 tsp sea salt

¼ tsp white pepper

Prep all your vegetables and construct your salad. Whisk the salad dressing ingredients together until they are emulsified. Serve together.

Mosaic of Beets & Radishes
with Horseradish Dressing

Serves 6 to 8

From the extravagant to the simple; you'll need a mandoline for this, or a steady hand and a sharp knife. The slimmer the slices, the prettier this plate can be. If you can find multicolored radishes in white, pink, red, purple, and black, all the better. Radishes were originally black, then bred to be red; same with carrots, which were originally purple and then bred to be orange—something to do with the royal family in the Netherlands.

½ cup [100 g] superfine sugar

2 Tbsp sea salt

Scant 1 cup [200 ml] red wine vinegar

2 red beets, peeled

2 golden and/or pink beets, peeled

About 12 whole multicolored radishes, very thinly sliced

For the dressing:

Scant ¼ cup [50 ml] of the drained beet pickling juice (see above)

Scant ¼ cup [50 ml] olive oil

1 tsp sea salt

2 in [5 cm] fresh horseradish root, peeled and finely grated, or a smear of wasabi paste

2 Tbsp poppy seeds

For the garnish:

¼ cup [30 g] nibbed pistachio nuts

Seeds of ½ pomegranate

In a medium saucepan, heat the sugar and salt with the vinegar until dissolved. Then add the whole beets and enough water to cover them. Cook over medium-low heat for 40 minutes, or until tender.

Remove the cooked beets from the cooking liquid using a slotted spoon and set aside to cool, reserving the liquid. Put half the radish slices in some of the beet cooking juices. After half an hour, they will be pink.

Cut the cooled beets into fine slices. Arrange some in overlapping layers in the middle of a large, round plate. Arrange the radish slices and remaining beet slices in concentric circles around the plate.

Mix the dressing ingredients together and drizzle over the salad. Dot with bright green pistachio nibs and blood-red pomegranate seeds.

Green Papaya & Zucchini Fettuccine with Cellophane Noodles & Cashews

Serves 4

4¼ oz [120 g] cellophane noodles

2 zucchini, julienned

1 green papaya, peeled, seeded, and julienned

Handful of cashew nuts, lightly toasted

1 red chile, very finely chopped

1 garlic clove, minced

1½-in [4-cm] piece of ginger, peeled and very finely chopped

1 Tbsp coconut palm sugar

1 Tbsp soy sauce

Juice of 1 lime

3 Tbsp peanut oil

Mint and cilantro leaves

Sea salt

We can learn from everyone's diet, even if it is not one we would want to follow on a permanent basis. Using raw vegetables to make "fettuccine" is a trick from the raw food/paleo songbook; a carb-free diet.

For this you will need either a julienne peeler or a machine called a "spiralizer." Raw-food-arians love their spiralizer machines! With these, all kinds of vegetables can be turned into noodle-thin strands that you can eat instead of pasta. Like the Chinese, I like to incorporate different textures into my food.

Soak the cellophane noodles in hot, salted water for 15 minutes, then drain them well.

Mix the zucchini, papaya, noodles, and cashews together. Make the dressing by pounding together, with a mortar and pestle or in a blender, the chile, garlic, ginger, sugar, and soy sauce. Add the lime juice and oil and stir into the zucchini, papaya, and noodles. Garnish with mint and cilantro leaves and serve.

Lettuce Cups with "Ceviche" & Sweet Potato

Serves 4 to 6

Hearts of palm have a similar structure and texture to crab sticks. Use these for a "ceviche" salad in Baby Gem leaves. Also good as a canapé before dinner. When I was traveling in Peru, I often had ceviche at roadside stands, served with a sweet potato. The starchiness perfectly complemented the citrusy ceviche. I'd use it to mop up the juices. (Photo on page 76.)

2 large sweet potatoes, peeled

2 Baby Gem lettuces, leaves separated

14-oz [400-g] can of hearts of palm, drained and rinsed

¼ red onion, finely diced

4 in [10 cm] celery stalk, finely sliced into little crescents

2 cherry tomatoes, thinly sliced

1 jalapeño or green chile, seeded and very finely chopped

Juice of 1 lime

1 tsp sweet paprika

Heaping 3 Tbsp [50 ml] Vegan Mayonnaise (see page 32)

1 ripe avocado, peeled, pitted, and diced

Sea salt

Handful of cilantro leaves, to serve

Boil the sweet potatoes in salted water in a medium saucepan for about 20 minutes until cooked. Drain and leave to cool, then cut into quarters.

Pick out the baby gem lettuce leaves that form a little bowl rather than the tiny leaves at the end, and arrange on a serving dish or plate.

Slice the hearts of palm in half lengthwise, then cut into ¼-in [6-mm] crescents. Put into a bowl and add the onion, celery, tomatoes, and chile. Season with some of the lime juice, the paprika, and salt to taste. Add the vegan mayonnaise and mix well. Finally, add the avocado and squeeze over some more lime juice.

Scoop the ceviche into the lettuce leaves and arrange the sweet potatoes on the serving dish or plate. Scatter with the cilantro and serve.

Pomelo, Chile, Peanut, & Cilantro Salad

Serves 2

1 pomelo, peeled and segmented

1 small red onion, finely sliced

3 scallions, sliced into thin rounds

⅜ cup [50 g] peanuts, crushed

Handful of cilantro leaves

Handful of mint leaves

Handful of Thai sweet/holy basil leaves (optional)

For the dressing:

Heaping 3 Tbsp [50 ml] peanut oil

4 tsp [20 ml] sesame oil

Juice of 2 limes

1 red bird's eye chile, seeded and finely diced

2 tsp sugar

1 tsp sea salt

¾-in [2-cm] piece of ginger, peeled and very finely chopped

I have a slight obsession with citrus—it's so much more interesting than just oranges and lemons. Recent discoveries I've made within the citrus family include Meyer lemons, Bengali limes (large, green knobbly fruit), bergamot (used in Earl Grey tea), pomelos, and yuzu. Some of these fruits are fragrant, and just one will transform a dish. I always nab a few blood oranges or Seville bitter oranges, in season in January, for gorgeous crimson-bleeding salads or to make my yearly marmalade. With a citrus salad one tends to go a bit Asian, but there is also the classic Italian combination of Sicilian blood orange and thinly sliced fennel.

Pomelos are enormous grapefruit-style fruits that you can often buy in Asian shops. If you can't get hold of one, feel free to use pink grapefruit. This is very refreshing.

First dot the pomelo segments around the plate, then add the rest of the ingredients. Whisk together the dressing ingredients, and pour it over the salad.

Vietnamese Summery Rolls

Makes 8

- 3½ oz [100 g] vermicelli rice noodles
- 10 round rice paper wrappers (includes 2 extras so that you can practice!)
- 16 button mushrooms, each sliced into 4 thin slices
- 12 to 16 baby lettuce leaves
- ½ cucumber, cut into thin, 1½-in [4-cm] long batons
- 2 carrots, peeled and cut into thin, 1½-in [4-cm] long batons
- 3 scallions, halved lengthwise and cut into 2-in [5-cm] sections
- 1¾ cups [100 g] bean or alfalfa sprouts
- Handful each of cilantro and mint leaves
- Handful of Thai sweet/holy basil leaves (or ordinary basil)
- 1 to 2 red chiles, finely diced
- Borage flowers, cornflowers (pink or blue) and marigold petals

For the dipping sauce:

- 3 Tbsp [50 ml] soy sauce
- Squeeze of lime juice

Options: instead of rice paper wrappers, you can use sturdy salad leaves such as Swiss chard with the above fillings, or with more Westernized fillings like hummus (see page 47) with julienned carrots or radishes.

These crunchy, fresh herby rolls from Vietnam are great picnic standbys, particularly if you have gluten-free guests. Think of them as little transparent windows of goodness. The bottom layer of filling, which will be turned over when finished, should be artfully arranged, as it will be visible through the wrapper. Once you get the hang of rolling them up, you'll return to this recipe regularly. On the photo shoot, food stylist Alice had the idea of adding delicate edible flowers, like eating a summer garden.

Soak the rice noodles in boiling water for 10 minutes until soft, then drain and cool.

Set up an assembly line, with several small bowls for the filling ingredients, and one large bowl of hot water to soak the rice paper wrappers, with 1 or 2 soaking at a time. Lay a clean dish towel on the counter.

Take one soaked, soft rice paper wrapper and lay it carefully on the dish towel. Place 8 mushroom slices in a row, one-third of the way up the rice paper wrapper, leaving a space at either end for folding.

Taking care not to overfill the roll, add 1 or 2 baby lettuce leaves, then a couple of batons of cucumber and carrot, some scallions, and bean sprouts or alfalfa. Add some herbs and a few strands of rice noodles. Sprinkle the diced chile on the rest of the rice wrapper, along with a few pretty leaves and the edible flowers.

Fold over the sides into the center, then roll up tightly, gathering in as you go and folding in the ends, finally rolling the whole thing into a cylindrical shape. Place seam side down, so they aren't touching, and cover with plastic wrap until you have assembled them all.

For the dipping sauce, mix the ingredients together. Arrange the summery rolls on a serving dish and dip in the sauce.

Plantain Fritters with Coconut & Cilantro Dip

Serves 6 to 8

I used to hang out with squatters in Hackney, east London. They often used to go "dumpster diving." I was living in the London Fields public outdoor swimming pool. Squatters get a bad rep, but actually they keep buildings alive. The London Fields pool was going to be turned into a parking lot by Hackney Council, but the squatters stayed there, heated it, repaired it, and when the council said they were going to turn it back into a swimming pool, left peaceably.

It was great fun living in the middle of a beautiful London park. There was a street full of squatters, all of whom had lived in these abandoned houses for longer than 12 years. This meant that they had the right to stay there. (The law has changed now.) I used to visit a local squatter family with my daughter. They were very alternative: home-schooled their kids, refused to have a car, made their own wine and alcohol, grew their own weed, cooked from scratch, and ate very good food. They even roasted their own coffee from green beans obtained from Ethiopia. Rob, the husband, made this dish, which I loved. He'd cycle to the local Ridley Road market where Caribbean food was sold.

Make sure you buy ripe—that is, yellow—plantains, not green. Normal bananas won't work, as their texture isn't as sturdy.

2 large, ripe yellow plantains, peeled

1 green chile, finely sliced

3 Tbsp all-purpose flour

3 cups [50 g] cilantro leaves

Rice bran oil, for deep-frying

Sea salt

For the dip:

1 fresh coconut

1 green chile, finely sliced

Juice of 2 lemons

Thumb of ginger, peeled and very finely chopped

3 cups [50 g] cilantro leaves

Mash the plantains by hand or in a food processor. Add the chile, flour, cilantro, and some salt.

For the dip, prepare the coconut as described on page 18. Using a powerful blender such as a Vitamix, process the coconut flesh and milk, chile, lemon juice, ginger, cilantro, and some salt.

Heat about ⅜ to ¾ in [1 to 2 cm] oil in a deep skillet. You can use any vegetable oil, but rice bran oil is very good with this recipe. Prepare a bowl with paper towels to absorb the oil. When a crumb dropped into the oil sizzles, the oil is hot enough. Use a tablespoon to scoop the plantain mixture into the oil. Continue until you have run out of room in the pan or until the mixture is used up. After a few minutes, turn over the fritters. When both sides are golden brown, remove to the paper towels to drain. Serve hot with the dip.

Cumin & Onion Farinata

Serves 4 to 6 (makes 3)

Farinata is a gluten-free, thick pancake made with gram flour (chickpea flour). In the south of France, you may know it as "socca." I first had it in Turin when I attended a Pink Bloc tactical frivolity protest against Berlusconi.

It wasn't all political action though, because, being at heart a *bourgeoise gourmande*, I managed to include some activities such as tasting the ice creams of several gelaterias, attending a chocolate festival in the center of town and trying the fudgy slices of farinata sold at the local bakery. Which was a useful foodstuff, as half the London samba band were either celiac, vegan, or freegan. I made the farinata with onions and cumin to give it a slightly Middle Eastern vibe. Combined with tabboulch; it made for a light and healthy weekend lunch.

Scant 3¼ cups [400 g] gram (chickpea) flour

1¼ cups [300 ml] water

⅔ cup [140 ml] olive oil

1 Tbsp ground cumin

1 Tbsp sea salt

2 onions, finely sliced

Olive oil, for frying

Mix the gram flour, water, and a generous 3 Tbsp [50 ml] of the olive oil together and leave for 2 to 12 hours, or overnight. Afterwards, add the cumin and salt.

Cook the onion slices in 3 Tbsp [45 ml] of the olive oil in a skillet over low heat until caramelized. This will take at least 15 to 20 minutes. Transfer to a plate.

Preheat the broiler to hot. You will need an ovenproof skillet, ideally cast iron. Even more ideally, you will have 2 of these, so that you can make 2 farinata at once!

Heat half of the remaining olive oil in the skillet, and add enough batter to cover the bottom of the pan so that it is about ⅝ in [1.5 cm] thick. Add the caramelized onions, and once the bottom seems done, or set, place the whole skillet under the hot broiler.

Leave until brown on top and slightly crispy at the edges. You can then start on the second one, using the remainder of the oil to grease the pan first.

Cut the farinata into slices like a pizza to serve.

Canary Island–Style Tempero Salt-Baked Mini Potatoes

Serves 4 to 6

18 oz [500 g] each
of three different
varieties/colors of
small heirloom potatoes
(3¼ lb/1.5 kg total)

2¼ lb [1 kg] tempero salt
(see page 19), rock salt
or sel gris

**For the tofu and pink
pepper cream:**

7 oz [200 g] silken tofu,
drained

⅜ cup [50 g] cashew nuts

1 preserved lemon, finely
chopped

1 tsp sea salt

To serve:

1 Tbsp pink peppercorns

Balsamic caviar pearls
(optional)

Baking things on salt is very Spanish. It has
the effect of wrinkling the skins, making the
inside very fluffy and the outside very crispy,
and at the same time seasoning the potato.

I used small heirloom potatoes from Carroll's
(www.heritage-potatoes.co.uk), where you
can buy 1.5-kg bags of red potatoes such as
Highland Burgundy and blue potatoes such as
Salad Blue, which have brightly hued interiors.
In fact, you could have a very patriotic dish
if you combined it with a white potato such
as Golden Wonder or Mayan Gold. Some of these
varieties are in season from October onwards,
but the rest of the year you could use purple
Albert Bartlett potatoes, which are purpley-
blue inside, and red-skinned potatoes, which
are white in the interior.

This can be a light lunch, served with salad,
or a canapé before dinner.

Preheat the oven to 400°F [200°C].

Wash the potatoes, leaving the skins on,
then dry them. Spread the salt onto a
roasting pan. Arrange the potatoes on
the salt, pricking each one, and bake
for 45 minutes.

To make the tofu and pink pepper cream,
mix all the ingredients together in a
blender. If you want it thicker, put
into a cheesecloth-lined strainer and
let it drain.

Remove the roasting pan from the oven, and
with a knife, cut a slit down the top of
the skin of each potato. Put a quenelle or
scoop of tofu cream onto each potato, with
a few pink peppercorns and some balsamic
pearls, if using, on top. Serve hot on the
bed of salt.

Agedashi Tofu in Broth

Serves 4

14 oz [400 g] silken
   tofu, drained

1½ cups [150 g]
   cornstarch

½ tsp fine sea salt

½ tsp finely ground
   white pepper

Oil, preferably peanut,
   for deep-frying

For the tentsuyu sauce:

1¼ cups [300 ml] dashi
   (see page 28)

4 Tbsp soy sauce

3 Tbsp sake

2 Tbsp mirin

1 Tbsp sugar

To serve:

4-in [10-cm] piece of
   daikon radish, peeled
   and grated

Thumb of ginger, peeled
   and grated

2 scallions, green part
   only, thinly sliced

This is one of my favourite Japanese
dishes: fried silken tofu in a delicate
broth. The Japanese technique for
cutting silken tofu is to put it in your
hand and cut it directly on the palm.

Cut the tofu into 2 to 2½-in [5 to
6-cm] cubes. Blot each piece with
paper towels. Season the cornstarch
with the salt and pepper and toss
the tofu cubes in it to coat.
Set aside.

Place all the ingredients for the
tentsuyu sauce in a small saucepan
and simmer over low heat. Do not
let it boil.

Heat up the oil for deep-frying in
a wok or a deep skillet. The oil is
ready when a cube of bread dropped
in rises to the surface and turns
golden after about 1 minute. Deep-
fry the tofu squares for about 6
minutes until they turn pale golden
or crispy. Remove with a slotted
spatula and place on a plate lined
with paper towels.

To serve, place a few pieces of
tofu in a small bowl and pour some
tentsuyu sauce around the tofu. Top
with the grated daikon, ginger and
scallions. Serve immediately.

3 Kinds Of Slider With All The Fixin's

Serves 8 to 12

The variety of recipes for veggie burgers is never-ending, but generally requires some kind of legume. Buy buns and squares of vegan melty cheese. Make sure you have Pink Pickled Onions (see page 14), relishes, and ketchup too.

Classic Bean Slider

Makes 8 sliders or 4 large burgers

2¼ cups [400 g] cooked beans (kidney beans are a good choice)

2 cups [80 g] panko or sourdough bread crumbs

2 Tbsp olive oil

2 chia or flax "eggs" (see page 21)

1 Tbsp English mustard

1 Tbsp nutritional yeast

Handful of chopped parsley

Squeeze of lemon juice

Oil, for frying

Sea salt and freshly ground black pepper

To assemble:

See Smoked Tofu Slider (page 108)

Preheat the oven to 350°F [180°C].

Combine all the ingredients and form into 8 sliders or 4 large burgers. In an ovenproof skillet, fry on each side in a little oil, until slightly golden. Transfer to the oven and cook for 7 to 10 minutes for sliders or 12 to 15 minutes for burgers. Warm the burger buns in the meantime.

Assemble as for the Smoked Tofu Slider (see page 108).

Sweet Potato Falafel Slider

Makes 10 to 12 sliders or 6 to 8 large burgers

1 sweet potato (about 9 oz [250 g]), skin on

4 garlic cloves, unpeeled

14-oz [400-g] can of chickpeas (garbanzo beans), or ⅔ cup [100 g] dried chickpeas, soaked overnight

2 tsp coriander seeds, ground

2 tsp cumin seeds, ground

1 onion, diced

2 green chiles, seeded and finely chopped

Handful of flat-leaf parsley, leaves chopped

Handful of cilantro, leaves chopped

Sea salt and freshly ground black pepper

Pita breads

Tahini

Slices of cucumber

Slices of red onion

Chili sauce

Preheat the oven to 400°F [200°C].

On a baking sheet, roast the sweet potato for 30 to 40 minutes, adding the garlic 15 minutes before the end. Then remove from the oven and let cool. Skin the sweet potato and garlic cloves. Reduce the oven temperature to 350°F [180°C].

Put the drained chickpeas (garbanzo beans), spices, onion, chiles, herbs and 1 Tbsp salt in a food processor, with pepper to taste. (I find a blender like a Vitamix makes the mixture too smooth and fine-grained for falafel.) Process until combined, then form the mixture into 10 to 12 sliders or 6 to 8 large burgers and place on a silicone baking mat.

Bake for 15 to 20 minutes for sliders or 20 to 30 minutes for burgers, flipping them halfway through. Warm the pita breads.

Assemble each by adding 1 Tbsp tahini, some cucumber and red onion slices, the falafel slider and chili sauce.

Smoked Tofu Slider

Makes 12 sliders or 6 large burgers

¾ cup [100 g] sunflower seeds

5 Tbsp pumpkin seeds

3 slices stale bread, made into bread crumbs

1 garlic clove, peeled

8 oz [225 g] smoked tofu, drained

3½ oz [100 g] firm tofu

1 Tbsp vegetable bouillon powder

1 Tbsp soy sauce

½ tsp thyme leaves

½ tsp white pepper

Oil, for frying

Sea salt

To assemble, for each patty:

1 burger bun

1 scoop of Vegan Mayonnaise (see page 32)

1 large romaine lettuce leaf

1 large slice of tomato

1 vegan cheese slice

Couple of slices of sweet pickled cucumber

Ketchup

Preheat the oven to 350°F [180°C].

Put the seeds, bread crumbs and garlic into the bowl of a food processor fitted with an S-blade and process until the mixture is coarsely ground, but still retains some texture (it's okay to see a few whole sunflower seeds in there).

Add the remaining ingredients except the oil, and process until the mixture comes together. Don't process for too long; you want to keep some texture from the seeds. Form into 12 sliders or 6 large burgers (this is easier if your hands are wet).

Heat a little oil in a skillet, add the sliders and fry on both sides until golden. Warm the buns in the meantime.

Split the buns, add the "vegannaise," then the lettuce leaf, tomato slice, patty, cheese slice, the pickle and some ketchup. Top with the other bun half and serve.

Onion Rings

Serves 6

This is a side for your sliders. I love sides; I could have a whole meal of sides. I have meat-eating mates who apologize to me when we go to restaurants because I can "only" have the sides from the menu. Typically meat-centric way of thinking. I'm happy with sides. Really, tapas are sides; small plates are sides. Long live sides.

1 qt [1 L] vegetable oil, for deep-frying

1¾ cups [160 g] tempura or cake flour

⅔ cup [160 ml] cold sparkling water

6 cups [150 g] cornflakes

1 Tbsp sweet smoked paprika

1 Tbsp sea salt

1 large onion, sliced into ¼-in [6 mm] thick rings

Chipotle Vegan Mayonnaise (see page 32) or ketchup, to serve

Heat the oil in your deep-fat fryer to 375°F [190°C]. In a bowl, combine the flour and sparkling water without over-stirring; the odd lump is fine. Crush the cornflakes so that they resemble large bread crumbs, then mix with the paprika and salt. Dip each onion ring into the batter mixture, then into the cornflakes. Deep-fry in batches until golden and crispy.

Dip into Chipotle Vegan Mayonnaise or ketchup and serve.

Ramen Hacks

Serves 1

Sometimes when I can't be bothered to cook, I buy instant noodles. They're quick; they're easy. But, buy good-quality package noodles; I have it on good authority that the best instant noodles are made by the Koreans. They are "bouncier." I chuck out the little packages of powdered vegetable/MSG and sesame oil, make a quick stock, and do my own toppings. Here are a few ideas.

Ramen originally derived from Chinese cooking, but took off in Japan after the First World War only after being made less Chinese and more Japanese, adding miso and making it less greasy, more delicate. Ramen is almost like a religion in Japan; everybody has their favorite noodle shop. Check out a very funny 1980s Japanese film called *Tampopo* to find out more. Today, ramen are called "doll" noodles by many Chinese, as the first manufacturers had a picture of a Japanese doll on the package. In Japan, they are now bringing out "feminine" ramen with less salt and MSG, as the biggest consumers are men aged between 20 and 40. Lazy so-and-sos!

- -

1 1 packet of ramen

2 Boiling water

3 Own stock, adding one of the following:

2 Tbsp mushroom miso (kinoko)

2 Tbsp miso

1 Tbsp vegetable bouillon powder

4 Add one or all of these flavorings:

1 Tbsp sesame oil

1 Tbsp soy sauce

½ tsp minced garlic

¾-inch [2-cm] piece of ginger, peeled and very finely chopped

½ tsp Sichuan peppercorns, ground

1 Tbsp black bean sauce

Squeeze of lime

5 Then add one or more of these toppings:

Small handful of shredded Napa cabbage

2 to 3 stalks of Chinese greens, such as bok choy

4 to 5 baby spinach leaves

Handful of sliced mushrooms, such as shiitake

3 to 4 slices of tofu, firm, smoked, or silken

1 Tbsp peanuts

5 to 6 strips of nori seaweed

Small handful of bean sprouts

2 to 3 scallions, chopped

2 Tbsp bamboo shoots, fermented (menma)

6 Finish with one or more of these garnishes:

Handful of cilantro leaves

Large pinch of pickled ginger

2 Tbsp Baechu Kimchi (see page 23)

1 Tbsp sesame seeds

Place the ramen into a largeish ceramic or wooden bowl. Pour boiling water onto your stock base, then pour this over the ramen. Add the flavorings. Then add the toppings. Leave for a few minutes until the ramen is soft. Add the garnish.

Mini Bunny Chows

Serves 4 to 6

5 peaches, not too
 ripe

Coconut or vegetable
 oil, for frying

1 Tbsp mustard seeds

1 cinnamon stick

1 bay leaf

5 green cardamom pods

2 cloves, ground

1 tsp ground cumin

1 tsp coriander seeds

1 large onion, diced

3 garlic cloves,
 minced

Thumb of ginger,
 peeled and very
 finely chopped

1 red chile, finely
 sliced

1 Tbsp ground turmeric

3½ oz [100 g] creamed
 coconut (half a
 7-oz [200-g] block

Scant 1½ cups
 [350 ml] hot water

10 small red potatoes,
 skin on, quartered

3 tomatoes, roughly
 chopped

½ red bell pepper,
 seeded and sliced

⅜ cup [50 g] golden
 raisins

4 to 6 crusty rolls

Handful of cilantro
 leaves

1 lime, cut into
 quarters

Sea salt

Bunny chow is similar to the trenchers that medieval Britons used. Prior to the generalized use of cutlery, trenchers were carriers for food and made from stale hollowed-out loaves. The advantage being that once a sauce had softened the bread, you could supplement the dish by tearing off and eating some of the trencher.

Bunny chow is a South African street food, specifically from Durban, and part of its "rainbow cuisine," with influences from indigenous tribal cooking, Malaysian, British, Afrikaans/Dutch and Indian food. It is filled with a curry. I served mini bunny chows at my South African supper club as a starter. It's a bit like a curry sandwich, very addictive, and a great lunch.

The piece of bread that remains from the hollowing-out process is referred to as a "virgin." Most bunnies are made from the ends of a quarter loaf of bread, but ones made from the middle of the loaf, without a crust at the bottom, are called "funny bunnies."

Cut a cross in the top of each peach and blanch in boiling water for 1 minute. Peel, remove the pit and cut into small dice.

Heat some oil in a medium saucepan over medium heat. First sling in the mustard seeds and wait until you hear them pop. Add the cinnamon stick, bay leaf, cardamom, cloves, cumin, and coriander. The secret to a good curry is a mix of whole and ground spices. Here you are tempering them, i.e., frying them before you add the rest of the ingredients, but only slightly, as you don't want everything to taste bitter.

Add the onion, garlic, ginger, chile, and turmeric. Then dissolve the creamed coconut in the hot water and stir into the curry. Add the potatoes and cook for 10 minutes. Add the tomatoes and red bell pepper, then the peaches and golden raisins, with salt to taste.

Cut the tops off the rolls and gut them, pulling out the centers. Scoop the curry inside, scatter over cilantro leaves and squeeze lime juice over. Put the cap back on. Eat while looking outside the window at the rain and think of Africa. Also very good the next day!

Dinner

This chapter contains more substantial meals for evenings, dinner parties, special occasions, and weekends. The recipes range from complicated, for those of you who want a challenge and have some time to try new techniques, to simple, throw-together meals. Vegan food is ethical, inspirational, colorful, cruelty-free, and, above all, delicious. Here is the proof of concept.

Fluffy Couscous

Serves 2 to 4

1½ cups [250 g] whole-wheat couscous

1 to 2 Tbsp sea salt

1 cup [250 ml] warm water

1 tsp ground ginger

1 tsp coriander seeds

1 tsp ground cumin

1 chile

4 to 5 dates or dried apricots, torn into pieces

1 Tbsp coconut oil

1½ Tbsp [20 g] nibbed pistachio nuts

1½ Tbsp [20 g] dried or semi-dried barberries or currants

2 Tbsp black poppy seeds

1 tsp ground cinnamon

1 Tbsp rosewater

2 Tbsp oil, ideally argan, for its subtly nutty taste

1 Tbsp bitter orange peel (optional)

Handful of pomegranate seeds (optional)

This is a step-by-step guide to the best way of making couscous. It's a bit fiddly and requires that you eschew such blasphemies as quick-cook couscous. But with this method, each grain will lift and separate just like a Playtex bra. No clumps, no sogginess. So, this weekend, have a go at making couscous from Northern Africa. I've combined it here with spices, and sweet and sour flavors. The idea is to reproduce that Middle Eastern vibe of fruity acidic tastes in a savory dish. If you don't have dates or dried apricots, use golden raisins; if you can't find nibbed pistachios, use almonds; you can riff on my recipe. Enjoy with the tagine opposite and a heavy Middle Eastern wine, such as Sidi Brahim.

Spread the couscous onto a flat tray. Add the salt to the warm water and let it dissolve. Then, using your fingers, sprinkle the couscous with the water and rub it through your fingers, not letting it clump. Do this twice more, every 15 minutes. You will see that the grains have plumped up nicely without sticking together or getting waterlogged.

You will need a fine-mesh strainer, plus a saucepan with a tight-fitting lid. (Or use a couscoussière if you have one; I don't.) Put almost boiling water into the saucepan, deep enough so that it won't steam away, but not so deep that it touches the strainer. Add the ginger, coriander seeds, cumin, and chile to the water.

Place the strainer over the pan and put your plumped-up couscous into the strainer with the dates or dried apricots. Wrap the lid in a clean dish towel and fit it onto the saucepan.

Place over medium heat for 15 to 20 minutes to steam, checking the water level occasionally so that it doesn't boil dry.

When the couscous is cooked, pour it into a bowl and mix in the coconut oil, pistachios, barberries, poppy seeds, cinnamon, rosewater, argan oil, and bitter orange peel, if using. Garnish with the pomegranate seeds, if using.

Carrot, Pepper, & Lentil Tagine

Serves 6

3 red bell peppers

5 Tbsp olive oil

2 onions, sliced

3 garlic cloves, minced

1 tsp ground cumin

½ tsp ground ginger

1 cinnamon stick

5 carrots, peeled and
thickly sliced

1 Tbsp orange flower water

1 Tbsp golden raisins

Heaping 1 cup [200 g]
dried red lentils

Pinch of saffron strands,
ground

2 cups [500 ml] vegetable
stock

Juice of ½ lemon

1 Tbsp ras el hanout
spice mix

12 black olives, pitted

12 dried apricots,
snipped into strips

Handful of sprigs of
flat-leaf parsley,
leaves picked

For the garnish:

Parsley and mint leaves
and/or dried rose
petals

2 preserved lemons,
sliced

Drizzle of argan oil

A tagine is both a method of cooking and a kind of Moroccan stewpot shaped like a cone. Condensation runs up the insides and back down into the food. If you don't have one, you can use a shallow casserole dish with a lid or, as many modern North Africans use, a pressure cooker.

Preheat the oven to 400°F [200°C]. Place the peppers on a baking sheet and roast in the oven until the skin is puffy and blackened. Remove to a plastic food bag. Once cool enough to handle, strip the blackened skins from them, removing the seeds and stalks. Tear the peppers into strips. Reduce the oven temperature to 325°F [160°C] if using a casserole rather than a tagine or pressure cooker.

Place a tagine, flameproof casserole dish, or pressure cooker over medium heat. When hot, add the olive oil and then the onions and garlic. Sweat until softened, then add the remaining ingredients, one after the other, and stir well. If using a tagine, cover and cook for about 30 minutes (or follow the manufacturer's instructions and timings if using a pressure cooker). If using a casserole dish, cover and transfer to the oven to cook for 30 to 45 minutes.

Garnish with parsley and mint or dried rose petals, preserved lemons, and a drizzle of argan oil, and serve with couscous (see opposite).

Freekeh with Purple Sprouting Broccoli & Almonds

Serves 4 to 6

1⅓ cups [200 g] freekeh
(whole grain)

2 cups [500 ml] hot
vegetable stock

Scant ⅔ cup [70 ml] olive oil

1 onion, diced

2 garlic cloves, minced

1 cinnamon stick

1 Tbsp sumac

½ cup [50 g] blanched
almonds

7 oz [200 g] purple
sprouting broccoli,
trimmed

Sea salt

For the gremolata:

2 handfuls of curly parsley

1 to 2 garlic cloves, peeled

Grated zest of 1 lemon

**Variation: Rather than frying
the purple sprouting broccoli,
make raw broccoli or cauliflower
"couscous" by processing it in a
food processor. Let the freekeh
cool slightly once cooked, then
stir in 9 oz [250 g] broccoli or
cauliflower "couscous." Serves 8
as a big salad.**

In my ongoing project to "vary my grains"
I picked up a box of the brilliantly named
freekeh in my local ethnic shop.

Freekeh, when cooked, tastes nutty and new.
But this green grain, fresh wheat from
Arabia is as old as the hills and mentioned
in the Bible. It's good for diabetes and
contains more protein than rice or couscous.
I fried it in olive oil and onions, then
studded it with sprouting broccoli and
almonds, and topped it with gremolata.

In a bowl, soak the freekeh in the hot
stock for 10 minutes or so.

Heat the oil in a wide, shallow
saucepan or deep-sided skillet, add the
onion and fry until soft, then add the
garlic, cinnamon stick, sumac, almonds,
purple sprouting broccoli, and salt to
taste. Cook until the broccoli is a
little bit steamed, then add the soaked
freekeh, stirring all the while.

Put the gremolata ingredients into a
food processor (or use a hand-held
blender) and blitz until finely chopped.
Sprinkle it over the freekeh and serve.

Quinoa with Hazelnuts, Roasted Vegetables, & Basil

Serves 2 to 4

As I said opposite, I'm trying to eat different grains, not just pasta. Quinoa, pronounced "keenwa" (I'm sure y'all knew that, but I feel I have to keep repeating it), has recently attracted controversy because some investigative journalists think that evil vegans are pricing out poor Peruvian farmers* from eating their own crop. How non-animal eaters could be entirely responsible for this, I'm not sure.

Supermarkets are now doing mixes of bulgur wheat and quinoa, which makes a change from the usual. Quinoa comes in several colors from white, pink, brown, black, and red. The mix I used had red quinoa, which is nuttier and perhaps more flavorsome than the white more commonly found on grocery shelves. Quinoa isn't a grain, but a grass that contains healthy fat and proteins, and it tricks the appetite into thinking you've had a nice bowl of starch.

Try this; it's not "cheffy" but it is gorgeous tasting.

*I spent five months in Peru and Bolivia, mostly with Quechua-speaking villagers, and I didn't once have quinoa. We ate potatoes, rice, and "fideos" (macaroni). This was quite some time ago, in the early 90s, so maybe it wasn't popular then. It seems strange to claim that Andean dwellers now have a daily shortage of quinoa.

1 eggplant, halved lengthwise and cut into strips

1 large red bell pepper, seeded and finely sliced

6 to 10 baby carrots, tops trimmed, bottoms snipped

About 3 generous Tbsp [50ml] olive oil

1½ cups [250 g] quinoa

Scant ⅔ cup [75 g] hazelnuts

1 preserved lemon or lime, finely diced

Handful of basil leaves, rolled up together and finely sliced (this is a chiffonade)

Hazelnut oil, for drizzling

Sea salt

Preheat the oven to 400°F [200°C].

Put the eggplant, pepper, and carrots in a roasting pan, toss in enough olive oil to coat everything well, and add 2 tsp salt. Roast for about 15 minutes until the eggplant and pepper are soft with slightly crispy edges.

Meanwhile, rinse the quinoa in a strainer until the water runs clear. Use double the volume of water to quinoa—in this case 3 cups [720 ml] water—and put both in a medium saucepan with 1 tsp salt. Bring to a boil, then cook for about 20 minutes. Leave to stand for 5 minutes off the heat and with the lid on. Then uncover and fluff it up with a fork.

Toast the hazelnuts in a dry skillet for 5 minutes. Mix the roasted vegetables, quinoa, hazelnuts, preserved lemon or lime, and basil together, drizzle with hazelnut oil, season with salt to taste and serve.

Kasha & Bows

Serves 2 to 4

A Russian Jewish dish that I learned from my friend Iris when I lived in Los Angeles for a while, way back when. A young photographer, doing freelance work for the *LA Weekly*, I also worked the graveyard shift in a top photo lab. Finishing at 4 A.M., I'd go dancing to garage music and "Tainted Love" in downtown clubs, then meet up with Iris at Canter's Deli, which was open 24/7. I even met a dowdy-looking Bette Midler in the queue, lining up with everyone else. Usually I'd order a root beer float and a bagel, but one night, Iris, a Russian Jewish girl from the valley, spotted a dish in the "sides" section of the vast laminated menu. "Kasha and bows!" she exclaimed, "I was brought up on that." It was actually a very healthy and filling side dish that cost very little. Iris was one of the most beautiful girls I'd ever known: jet-black hair, pale blue, almond-shaped eyes and white skin. She spent a few years on heroin, which only made her pale eyes paler, for her pupils were tiny, and it made her skin even more alabaster in hue. She was like a punk Snow White.

I left the States after a couple of years—things got too murky. A girl was found dead in her apartment upstairs from mine. An escaped rapist broke into my apartment, but I managed to act crazy and scare him off. There were rats living behind my wide retro American fridge. It was time to go home.

I'm happy to report that Iris Berry is now a renowned poet, and still beautiful. This is her aunt's recipe for kasha and bows.

Kasha is the Russian name for buckwheat, which comes in 2 types: roasted and unroasted. The roasted is darker and nuttier. You can buy this at Eastern European stores. It's not actually a grain; it's in the beet family and is therefore low GI and gluten free (although the pasta bows are not).

⅔ cup [100 g] roasted kasha buckwheat groats

Scant 1 cup [200 ml] vegetable stock

3¾ cups [250 g] dried farfalle pasta (bows)

About 3 generous Tbsp [50 ml] olive oil

2 large onions, roughly chopped

4 garlic cloves, minced

Juice of 1 lemon

Sea salt and freshly ground black pepper

Parsley leaves, to garnish

Get 2 medium saucepans. In one cook the kasha with the vegetable stock (this should take about 15 minutes) and in the other cook the pasta in boiling, salted water (12 to 15 minutes depending on the brand) until al dente.

Heat the oil in a large skillet over medium-high heat, then add the onions and cook until soft and caramelized. Add the garlic and cook until soft. Finally, add the kasha (which should have absorbed virtually all the stock during cooking) and the drained bows. Cook, tossing, until heated through and coated in the oil and onions. Squeeze the lemon juice over, add salt and pepper to taste, garnish with parsley leaves, and serve.

Green Beans with Pink Soba Noodles, Miso, Pecans, Pink Pickled Ginger, & Purple Umeboshi Plums

Serves 4

I had something like this at a fantastic Japanese restaurant in Soho, London called Koya. Pink soba noodles are flavored with plums and you can also buy them in green (green tea-flavored), black or white. They cook very quickly and have no gluten (though you should check the label, as some soba noodles contain wheat). In this recipe, you eat them cold—sounds weird, huh? Actually it works: the hot beans, cold noodles, salty fudgy taste of nuts and miso, and vinegary heat of the ginger.

Soba noodles are the healthiest fast food; ready in minutes. If you are a bit dubious about the cold noodle thing, or unable to get hold of soba noodles, you could of course use any soft noodles for this, like rice or wheat (udon) noodles, which you can often buy ready-cooked, just necessitating a bit of heating up.

The pickled ginger can be bought in Asian shops or online. Here I'm talking about the dark pink shredded stuff rather than the salmon-pink slivers we find in sushi bars.

(Photo on page 114.)

7 oz [200 g] green beans (you can also use "wax beans," which are a paler color, or any combo of long beans)

1¼-in [3-cm] piece of fresh ginger, peeled and chopped

2 Tbsp miso

¾ cup [80 g] pecans

2 tsp soy sauce, or to taste

2 Tbsp rice wine vinegar

1 Tbsp mirin

1 Tbsp sesame oil

7 oz [200 g] pink soba noodles (check the label to make sure they are vegan)

4 Tbsp shredded dark pink pickled ginger

8 purple umeboshi plums

Sea salt

Bring a saucepan of water to a boil and add salt. Cook the beans for about 5 minutes until bright green and just tender. Drain and plunge into cold water, then drain again. Set aside in a bowl.

Put the fresh ginger, miso, pecans, soy sauce, rice wine vinegar, mirin and sesame oil in a food processor and grind together.

Then bring another medium saucepan of salted water to a boil and plunge in the pink soba noodles. They will cook quickly, —in about 5 minutes. Drain and rinse in cold water.

Toss the beans in the ginger pecan sauce and plate the noodles, piling the beans on top. Serve with dark pink pickled ginger and 2 umeboshi plums per person.

Fresh Vegan Pasta

Makes approximately 14 oz [400 g] fresh pasta, serves 2 to 4

This is more or less the same recipe as normal fresh pasta, but obviously without the egg. If you want yellow egg-like pasta, just add a little ground turmeric to the dough. It's important to get hard wheat (grano duro) pasta flour (00) because it will add gluten and stretchiness, which you need because you don't have the egg. You can make pasta with just oil and water, but I did find that the egg replacer introduced smoothness and stretchiness to the pasta dough.

If you can't get hold of 00 pasta flour, then use three parts white bread flour to one part all-purpose flour (i.e.: for 9 oz [250 g] use (rounding up) 1⅓ cups [190 g] white bread flour to a scant ½ cup [60 g] all-purpose flour).

9 oz [250 g] Italian 00 pasta flour

1 tsp sea salt

⅓ cup [75 ml] water

3 Tbsp olive oil OR 6 Tbsp [90 ml] water mixed with 1 tsp egg replacer

Fine semolina, for dusting

If mixing by hand, put the flour and salt into a bowl, make a well in the center and add the water and the oil, or water and egg replacer. Stir with a wooden spoon, then knead it together with your hands. Good pasta is all about texture; it mustn't be too dry or too wet. Form a ball, cover with plastic wrap, and leave to rest at room temperature for 30 minutes. The resting time is important, as this will make the dough more flexible.

If using a food processor, put the flour and salt in and slowly pulse in the water and the oil, or water and egg replacer. Stop when it looks like large couscous. Then remove the dough, form a ball and knead it by hand for several minutes until well combined. Continue as for by hand.

Once the dough has rested, divide in half. Use one half at a time, leaving the other half covered with plastic wrap or a damp clean dish towel as you work. If you have a pasta maker, run the ball through it on the widest setting. Then fold the dough over and run it through the machine several times, folding over each time and inserting the open end into the machine. Eventually you will see a bubble form and/or a popping sound as the folded end goes into the pasta machine. This means the pasta is now ready to roll.

Thread the flattened oval of pasta through the machine (no longer folding it over) on each setting, starting at the widest and narrowing it by one notch each time. By notch 5 you will probably have to cut your tongue of pasta in half, unless you have an assistant or unbelievably long arms. Continue to run the pasta through the machine and stop before the last notch (usually 7) because you don't want the dough so thin that it will break and leak the contents while cooking. Hang up the pasta tongues to dry (I use my wooden washing line! but you can buy wooden pasta dryers) for 10 to 15 minutes or so. However, you don't want it to dry too much or it will break.

If you don't have a machine, then roll the pasta out very thinly on a floured surface, making quarter turns as in pastry, until it is about $1/16$ in [2 mm] thick.

Then change the flat pasta roller on the machine for the shape of pasta you want to cut, or if you are making it without a machine, roll up the oval of dough loosely and make perpendicular cuts all along, every ¼ in [6 mm], so that you end up with coils of flat, thin pasta.

For ravioli, you can cut circles with a small glass, add the filling to one and press a second circle on top, brushing the edges with water and pinching them together (you can also buy several types of ravioli cutter in kitchen shops).

The second problem with pasta, once you have made it, is to stop it sticking. I sprinkle a thick layer of fine semolina on a tray and spread the pasta out on top. In fact, while I'm making long pasta shapes in the machine, I hold the tray underneath so that the pasta falls straight into the semolina flour. With finer pasta such as fettuccine, curl it into nests, liberally sprinkling with the semolina, and leave to air-dry for a day. If I'm not using it immediately, I freeze it on the tray (so choose a tray that fits into your freezer shelves). Once it is frozen, you can transfer it to a plastic freezer bag and store it for up to 3 months. Remember NEVER wash your pasta machine, otherwise it will go rusty. Clean it with a dry brush.

To cook the pasta, always add salt to a large saucepan of water and bring to a boil. Cook the pasta for 1 to 5 minutes until it floats to the surface. Ravioli can take a bit longer—5 to 10 minutes—but don't walk away from the stove!

Flower & Herb Pasta

Serves 4

I make edible geranium, dill, sage, and nasturtium noodles by adding these just before I start rolling the pasta. The flowers stretch, but it looks so pretty, like floral lisle stockings! Roll up loosely and cut wide noodles. Cook very quickly (3 to 5 minutes) in boiling, salted water and serve with olive oil, chopped fresh herbs, more flowers, pine nuts, and black pepper.

Kale Pesto

2½ to 3 cups [100 g] chopped kale or Tuscan black cabbage

Scant ⅔ cup [75 g] pine nuts

2 Tbsp nutritional yeast

3 garlic cloves peeled

Scant ½ cup [100 ml] olive oil

3 big Tbsp [50 ml] sunflower oil

2 Tbsp lemon juice

Sea salt

Cut the thick stems from the kale or Tuscan black cabbage and pull off the rest of the leaves.

Put the pine nuts, nutritional yeast, garlic, and kale into a food processor and whizz until finely chopped.

With the motor still running, drizzle in the oils and lemon juice. Add salt to taste.

Vegan Pesto Alla Genovese

This recipe from Genoa is traditionally made with basil and pine nuts, but there is also a *pesto alla trapanese*, from Trapani in Sicily, made with walnuts or almonds in place of the pine nuts.

Large bunch of basil, leaves only

1 garlic clove, peeled

⅜ cup [50 g] pine nuts

3 generous Tbsp [50 ml] olive oil

2 Tbsp nutritional yeast

Juice of ½ lemon

Sea salt

Pulse all the ingredients in a food processor until they form a paste. Add salt to taste.

Watercress & Lemon Zest Pesto

2 cups [100 g] watercress

Grated zest of 1 lemon

2 Tbsp pine nuts

3 Tbsp nut or olive oil

Freshly ground black pepper

Whizz the ingredients together in a food processor until combined. Add pepper to taste.

Chocolate Sichuan Pepper Fettuccine with Porcini & Black Olives

Serves 4

For the chocolate fettuccine:

9 oz [250 g] Italian 00 pasta flour

1 tsp sea salt, plus extra for cooking the pasta

1 tsp very finely ground Sichuan or other pepper

½ cup [50 g] cocoa powder

Scant ½ cup [115 ml] water

Generous ⅔ cup [165 ml] water mixed with 1 tsp egg replacer

Fine semolina, for dusting

For the sauce:

¼ cup [20 g] dried porcini

Scant ½ cup [100 ml] boiling water

Generous 3 Tbsp [50 ml] olive oil

3 shallots, thinly sliced

2 garlic cloves, minced

1 tsp sea salt

1¼ cups [100 g] fresh ceps or other wild or brown mushrooms, thinly sliced

12 pitted black olives

Juice of ½ lemon

Scant ½ cup [100 ml] soy cream

To serve:

Basil leaves

Freshly ground black pepper

Make the fettuccine following the instructions on page 122, and adding the pepper and cocoa powder at the same time as the flour and salt.

Cover the dried porcini with the boiling water and leave to soak for at least 30 minutes. Drain and reserve the soaking water.

Meanwhile, heat the oil in a medium skillet over medium heat, sweat the shallots, adding the garlic and salt, then add the fresh mushrooms and the olives. As the sauce reduces, gradually add the porcini soaking liquid until it develops a thickened, but pouring consistency. Add the lemon juice and leave to rest, then add the soy cream just before serving. (The sauce develops flavor if left a while.)

Fill a large saucepan with water and bring to a boil with at least 1 Tbsp sea salt.

Making sure the fettuccine is in separate strands before you put it in the water, drop it in the boiling water and be ready to scoop it out when it floats. Depending on how thick your pasta is, this can take only a minute.

Place the pasta in the middle of the dish and drape the sauce over it. Garnish with basil and black pepper.

Benign Dictatorship Saffron Spaghetti

Serves 6 with leftover sauce

This is my Death Row dish. I could pretty much eat this every day. Spaghetti Napoli or Napolitana—or spaghetti with tomato sauce—is simple and beautiful; a mainstay of my family life. Does it come from Naples? Yeah, probs. Southern Italy was, is, poorer and hotter than the north and so, not only were they growing ace tomatoes, but they could also not afford to add meat to their pasta sauce. Who needs meat when great tomatoes provide all the umami oomph you could possibly want? So "Bolognese" from Bologna (in northern Italy), the classic ground meat and tomato spaghetti sauce, became "Napolitana" (from the south), an infinitely chic-er dish.

Another reason for the popularity of the meatless sauce is that tomatoes used to be more acidic until it was bred out of them. A Napoli sauce was something you could preserve, conveniently bottled on long journeys, for the winter.

It's strange to think about the process of "nation branding" and how misleading it can be. I recently attended a talk where it was explained that the great English breakfast was only about 150 years old, invented, like so much else including Christmas, in the Victorian times. When we think about Italy and its "USP," we visualize the red, white, and green of the flag. The red is the tomato, the white is the pasta, and the green is the basil.

But the tomato is fairly new to Italy, arriving after the discovery of America, via Spain in the 16th century. Furthermore, pasta was reserved for feast days, only becoming regularly available to the poor when the manufacturing process was mechanized in the late 19th century.

Spaghetti Napoli was the second recipe I was ever taught by my mother. I'd decided, at a ridiculously early age, to host a dinner party for 15 people, with 3 courses. The dinner party was a bit of a disaster: starters went out at 11 P.M., I got far too drunk, and my best friend got off with the boy that this whole shenanigans was constructed for. But I learned how to make this dish, so it wasn't a write-off.

5 Tbsp olive oil, plus a large glug

2 onions, diced

4 to 5 garlic cloves, minced

5 bay leaves, ideally fresh

3 to 4 x 14-oz [400-g] cans or jars of tomatoes, or 2¼ lb [1 kg] fresh tomatoes

Large pinch of saffron strands

1 sprig of oregano (optional)

25 oz [700 g] good-quality dried spaghetti (I generally work on 3½ oz [100 g] cooked per person for a appetizer, 5¼ oz [150 g] cooked for a main course)

Sea salt and plenty of freshly ground black pepper

- -

This sauce is really simple if you follow my instructions exactly. Do not freestyle it, something I generally give you permission to do in other recipes. No, this is a benign dictatorship when it comes to spaghetti.

Before we start, a few rules:

1. On no account add sugar. The French add sugar, which is why they are terrible at pasta even if they are good at everything else. If you want a sweeter sauce, wait a day before eating it. It will become sweeter.

2. Buy the best tomatoes you can afford—fresh or canned. If you are buying canned tomatoes, DO NOT buy those watery cheap cans containing 3 flayed plum-shaped tomatoes and a load of thin red juice. Buy the most expensive. Hell, go crazy, save yourself some effort and buy ready-chopped.

Organic is good. I used Così
Com'è bottled tomatoes (yellow
and red) in this recipe, and
their flavor is extraordinary.
I don't care how poor you are,
I don't care if you have had
all your savings seized; you
can buy a halfway decent can
of tomatoes.

3. Buy the best spaghetti you can
   afford. NOT quick-cook. The
   longer the cooking time on
   the package, the better. Buy
   11-minute spaghetti, bronze-
   die preferably (this gives the
   surface a roughness that means
   the sauce adheres). If you buy
   very good pasta, it's almost
   impossible to overcook it.
   Brands I recommend: Barilla,
   De Cecco, Garofalo.

4. Salt your pasta water. Salt
   it until it is as salty as the
   Mediterranean Sea. With sea
   salt. If you have sufficiently
   seasoned your water, you will
   not need to add salt at the
   table. Geddit?

Heat the oil in a large pan, add
the onions and cook until soft.
Add the garlic and bay leaves.
Stir. Add the tomatoes. I tend
to squeeze the tomatoes, tearing
them as I go, into the pan (fresh
tomatoes I will chop up). Stir in
1 Tbsp salt, the saffron and
oregano, if using (if you have
fresh, but don't bother with out-
of-date dried oregano. In fact, go
through your spice cupboard, check
the dates and chuck most of it
out. In India, housewives buy small
quantities of fresh spices WEEKLY.
This is what we should be doing).

Simmer, uncovered, for 45 minutes
over low heat, if you have time.
It's pretty good after 20 minutes.
If I'm drinking red wine, I might

sling in half a glass if the sauce
is getting too concentrated.

The pasta bit:

Get a large or tall saucepan.
Don't use a small saucepan.
Really. It's the same as salads.
Why do people try to squash a
salad into a tiny bowl? You can't
toss the salad in the dressing!
So if you haven't got a big
pasta saucepan, it's time you
invested in one. It's about $50
for something you'll probably use
every day for the next decade.

Get a big load of salty boiling
water on the go. Boil 3 or 4
kettles if necessary and fill it
up that way. Throw in a handful
of sea salt. Yes: a handful. It's
fine, don't worry. Feel the fear
and do it anyway.

When it's bubbling, put the
spaghetti in, pushing down gradually
until it's all submerged. Stir a
couple of times during cooking to
keep the strands separate. Cook
for a minute less than they say
on the package and have your
colander ready in the sink.

Strain out the pasta quickly,
then dump it back into the hot
saucepan. Splash a large glug
of olive oil over the hot pasta,
stirring it, to prevent the pasta
sticking together.

If you are being mamma at the
table, have a stack of bowls, put
the lid on the pasta and take both
the pasta and the sauce to the
table. Serve into each bowl at the
table, pasta first, sauce on top.
Yes I know Jamie Oliver says add
the pasta to the sauce, but it
looks prettier this way and people
like different amounts of sauce.
Make sure there is a pepper mill
at the table.

Beet Pelmeni with Herb & Walnut Filling

Makes 80 to 90 pelmeni, serves 6 to 8

If you live near any Eastern European stores, buy a pelmeni mold (otherwise use a ravioli cutter or a pasta machine that has a ravioli cutter). This is a fusion of Polish pelmeni and a Georgian walnut stuffing.

10½ oz [300 g] cooked beets (or 3 tsp beet powder mixed with 1 Tbsp water)

1 tsp sea salt

4 cups [500 g] Italian 00 pasta flour

5 Tbsp olive oil

5 Tbsp warm water mixed with 1 Tbsp egg replacer

Extra pasta flour or fine semolina, for dusting

For the filling:

3 cups [300 g] walnuts

½ tsp coriander seeds

1 tsp ground marigold petals (organic, unsprayed)

1 tsp sea salt

2 garlic cloves, minced

Handful of cilantro leaves

Pinch of fenugreek seeds

1 Tbsp red wine vinegar

Small handfuls of mixed herbs, such as parsley, cilantro, pennyroyal, dill and tarragon

To serve:

A little walnut oil

Pomegranate seeds

Marigold petals

Put the cooked beets, if using, in a food processor and pulse to a purée. Add the salt.

Put the flour into a large bowl and make a well in the center. Pour in the beet purée and mix to a dough, then gradually add the olive oil, followed by the beet powder paste, if using, and the water and egg replacer, checking all the time to make sure you have just the right consistency for the pasta. (If using a food processor, add the hot water a tablespoon at a time with the machine running until the pasta forms large grains. Then knead together by hand.) Shape into a ball, cover with plastic wrap, and leave it to rest at room temperature.

In a powerful food processor, finely grind the walnuts. Transfer to a bowl and put the coriander seeds, marigold petals, salt, garlic, cilantro leaves and fenugreek in the processor. Whizz to a paste, then mix with the walnuts, vinegar, and mixed chopped herbs. (This paste, with added oil, also makes a good pesto.)

Divide the rested dough into 4 pieces, and work with one at a time, keeping the other pieces covered in plastic wrap so that they don't dry out. Roll out the dark pink dough as thinly as you can (or use a pasta machine —see the pasta recipe on page 122) to a circle slightly bigger than the pelmeni mold. Lay one sheet over the mold, then spoon ½ tsp filling mixture into each compartment. Lay another sheet of pasta on top, sealing with water and pressing firmly around the sides.

Transfer the pelmeni to a large baking sheet dusted with flour or semolina, making sure they are in a single layer. You can freeze them like this, then once frozen, they can be dumped into a plastic bag in the freezer.

Fill a large saucepan with boiling, salted water. Drop the fresh pelmeni into the boiling water and cook until they start to float. Make sure they don't overcook. Drain and serve with walnut oil, pomegranate seeds, and marigold petals.

Steamed Gyoza with Mushroom & Tofu Filling

Makes 24

This is basically an Asian version of ravioli, or to be historically accurate, the other way around, for pasta came from China. Buy the little circles of "pasta" from Chinese or Japanese shops, but check carefully that they don't contain egg. I made these gyoza in a wok that fitted my bamboo steamer just perfectly. A bamboo steamer is very cheap, or you can use a metal steamer. You need a flat surface, as you don't want to have the gyoza touching each other; they will stick and rip the skin off.

3 Tbsp sesame oil

2 garlic cloves, minced

Thumb of ginger, peeled and very finely chopped

1 Tbsp sugar

3 Tbsp dark soy sauce

1 tsp Chinese five-spice powder

1 tsp cornstarch

7 oz [200 g] firm tofu

4 scallions, sliced, white and green parts set aside separately

9 oz [250 g] shiitake or other mushrooms, finely sliced

1 package of 24 gyoza or Chinese wonton skins

Rice flour or all-purpose flour, for dusting

Plum sauce, to serve

Variation: Add finely chopped Baechu Kimchi (see page 23) to the filling.

To make the filling, put the sesame oil, garlic, ginger, sugar, soy sauce, five-spice powder and cornstarch into a hot wok or skillet and sizzle for a couple of minutes. Drain and dice the tofu, then add to the wok or pan and fry for 5 minutes. Add the white slices of scallion and the mushrooms and fry for 3 to 5 minutes (they will release a lot of liquid).

Place a strainer over a bowl. Transfer all the mixture into the strainer and let the excess liquid drain out (you don't want a very liquid filling, as the gyoza skins will not hold it).

Then set up a little gyoza filling station on a table: a small bowl of water, a stack of gyoza skins, the cooled filling and a teaspoon. Lay out a gyoza skin, dip your finger into the water and run it around the border of the gyoza skin. Put a heaping teaspoon of filling into the center, then bring up the sides and press them together to seal the gyoza like crescent-shaped dumplings.

Set aside each dumpling on a tray sprinkled generously with flour so that they won't stick to the bottom when you remove them to steam. When you have shaped them all, place in a steamer, spaced slightly apart. Take a piece of parchment paper and cut into the shape of your steamer. Run it under the faucet to moisten it.

Prepare a large pot or wok of boiling water and place the steamer over it. Put the circle of moist parchment paper over the gyoza, then put on the lid. Steam for about 20 minutes, depending on how fresh they are, and on the thickness of the skins. They are cooked when they are translucent. Then fry in a pan too, if you like. Serve with the reserved green scallion slices and the plum sauce for dipping.

Three-Topping Polenta Party

Serves 5

2½ qt [2.25 L]
water (for quick-
cook polenta use
only 6½ cups
[1.5 L]

1 Tbsp sea salt

3⅓ cups [500 g] fine
polenta

3 Tbsp olive oil

Three toppings:

Peperonata (below)

Artichokes in oil

Grilled fennel
slices

Variations:
Pesto (page 124),
caramelized onions
with garlic,
mushrooms in cashew
cream and garlic,
Napolitana sauce
(page 126), broiled
eggplant, braised
chicory, leeks,
cardoons

I made this at my vegan supper club with big-time vegan cookery author, Terry Hope Romero. Tickets sold out within a day. Interestingly, on the night, half our guests weren't vegan but vegan-curious meat eaters.

Boil the water in a large, good-quality, heavy-bottomed saucepan (you don't want a thin bottom on your cookware anyway). Add the salt and then the polenta. Keep stirring. With the slow-cook polenta, it can take 90 minutes. The quick-cook takes about 2 minutes. What's the difference? The slow-cook is a little more "corny," a little grittier and possibly better for a dinner party in that it stays soft for longer. You want a nice, thick soupy polenta that you can spoon onto a wooden board; not too thick, but not so thin that it runs off the board.

Spoon the polenta onto the board and spread it out. Drizzle with the olive oil and add the warmed toppings in stripes on top. Serve by giving everyone a spoon to help themselves. Fun and interactive!

Got leftover polenta? Cut into slices and broil. Serve for breakfast with diced jalapeños, tomatoes, onion, and cilantro salsa with plenty of lime juice.

Peperonata

Serves 2 to 4

Scant ½ cup [100 ml]
olive oil

7 Romano peppers

1 yellow bell pepper

1 onion, sliced

3 garlic cloves, minced

1 tsp sweet smoked paprika

1 Tbsp each chopped
marjoram and oregano

2 bay leaves

Glug of verjuice

2 Tbsp drained capers

1 Tbsp drained pickled green
peppercorns (optional)

Sea salt

Preheat the oven to 350°F [180°C]. Oil a baking pan with some of the oil. Put all the peppers on it whole, toss in more oil and roast for 15 to 20 minutes. Take them out, strip off the skins, remove the stalks and seeds and cut the flesh into ¾-in [2-cm] strips. Pour any tasty oil from the pan into a heavy, ovenproof pan with a lid and add more olive oil. Add the onion and sweat, without letting it burn; it should be soft. Add the garlic, paprika, 1 Tbsp salt, the herbs, and verjuice.

Add the pepper strips. Put the lid on and cook in the oven for 45 minutes. The peppers should be soft and sweet. Add the capers and peppercorns, if using, check the seasoning, and serve warm or cold.

Uthappam

Makes 8 uthappam

Uthappam is frequently referred to as a kind of Indian pizza, but having made it, it was more like large, shallow sub-continental crumpets. It's one of the best things I have made in ages. I chose to top it with onions fried in oil with mustard seeds and curry leaves.

First you must make the batter, which is a lengthy process, but it is important to make sure that it ferments to the right flavor and texture. You'll need to start prepping several days in advance of serving.

For the dhosa batter:

Scant 10 oz [275 g] broken or parboiled rice (available in Indian shops under these names)

½ tsp fenugreek seeds

Scant ½ cup [65 g] urad dhal (white lentils), skinless and preferably whole

1¼ cups [300 ml] water

1 tsp sugar

1 Tbsp sea salt

Vegetable oil, for frying

For the topping, per uthappam:

2 Tbsp vegetable or coconut oil

½ tsp cumin seeds

½ tsp mustard seeds

1 small onion, red or yellow, finely sliced into rings

1 green chile, thinly sliced

Large pinch of curry leaves, fresh or dried

Pinch of sea salt

For the dhosa batter, soak the rice and fenugreek in plenty of cold water for 12 hours. Thirty minutes before the end of the soaking, put the urad dhal separately in plenty of water to soak.

Drain the rice and dhal and grind really well together in a blender or food processor with the fresh water, in 2 batches (I use a Vitamix, which grinds very finely), until frothy, smooth and chalky.

Put the batter in a bowl and cover with a dish towel. Leave to ferment at room temperature (not in the fridge, unless you live in a hot country like India) for 3 to 4 days, checking every day. When it's bubbly and tastes a bit sour, it's fermented. This is very important, because if you cook the batter when it isn't sufficiently fermented, the uthappam will be heavy and tasteless. Stir in the sugar and salt.

For the topping, heat the oil in a small skillet. Add the cumin seeds, then the mustard seeds. Let them pop. Then add the onion, chile, and curry leaves and cook until the edges of the onion are golden and the centers are soft.

Heat a little oil in a tava (Indian frying pan) or flat pancake pan, then put in half a ladle of the dhosa batter. The batter circle should be about 3¼ to 4 in [8 to 10 cm] in diameter and ¼ in [6 mm] thick. Let the bottom cook (it will form air bubbles, like a crumpet), then spoon the onion mixture on top. Sprinkle over a pinch of salt and eat it all up. Then, probably, make another one and eat that all up too. Mmmm.

Pizzette with Roast Pumpkin, Red Onion, & Sage

Makes 2

For the dough:

1¾ cups [250 g] white bread flour

1 tsp sea salt

1 tsp active dry yeast

1 tsp superfine sugar

⅞ cup [200 ml] lukewarm water

1 Tbsp olive oil, plus extra for oiling

Fine semolina, for dusting

For the topping:

18 oz [500 g] pumpkin, seeded and sliced into crescents

1½ tsp sea salt

4 Tbsp olive oil, plus extra for drizzling

1 red onion, sliced

2 garlic cloves, minced

Handful of sage leaves

Grated zest of 1 lemon (optional)

I made these for an *Eat, Pray, Love* supper club, commissioned by the film distributors. The film's protagonist, played by Julia Roberts, was depressed even though she had a) a lovely husband b) a gorgeous lover c) a great job as a successful writer. She recovered by going to Italy and eating great pizza. In the film. I'm not sure Julia Roberts ever eats pizza irl. These pizzette have a seasonal, autumnally inspired topping. It's a great recipe for Halloween.

Preheat the oven to 400°F [200°C]. Place a large baking sheet in to heat up.

Put the flour and salt into a large bowl. Mix the yeast, sugar, and water in a pitcher and leave to bubble for about 5 minutes. Pour the yeast mixture into the flour and add the olive oil.

Mix together, then knead the dough on the work surface until smooth. (You can use a food processor up to this stage, if you prefer.) Put back in the bowl, cover, and leave to rest in a warm place for 1 hour.

In the meantime, toss the pumpkin slices and salt in the olive oil on a rimmed baking sheet. (You can peel the pumpkin slices, but I don't bother. The skin is quite thin and not unpleasant.) Roast for 15 to 20 minutes, or until soft and caramelized around the edges, then add the red onion and garlic and roast for another 10 minutes.

Transfer the risen dough onto an oiled surface, cut into 2 pieces and roll each piece into a circle. It doesn't matter if the circles aren't perfect—that's all part of the homemade look!

Then dust 2 pieces of baking parchment with semolina and place a dough circle on each. Arrange the pumpkin and onion over the pizzette, scatter sage leaves all over, and drizzle with olive oil.

Slide both pizzette, on their baking parchment, onto the hot baking sheet in the oven and bake for 10 to 12 minutes. Remove from the oven and sprinkle over the lemon zest, if using. Serve with a simple watercress salad.

Hibiscus Flowers in Blue Corn Enchiladas with Pickled Purple Cabbage

Serves 7 (2 enchiladas each)

For the filling:

3½ oz [100 g] dried or fresh hibiscus flowers

Generous 3 Tbsp [50 ml] olive oil

1 large onion, thinly sliced

3 garlic cloves, minced

2 large carrots, grated

Scant 1 cup [100 g] grated daikon radish

¼ cup [50 g] sugar

½ tsp dried oregano

¼ tsp dried thyme

Sea salt and freshly ground black pepper

For the pickled purple cabbage:

½ cup [100 g] sugar

Scant 2 Tbsp [20 g] sea salt

⅞ cup [200 ml] red wine vinegar

¼ red cabbage, very thinly sliced

For the chipotle tomato sauce:

2 Tbsp vegetable oil

1 white onion, sliced

3 fresh bay leaves

1 Tbsp fresh or dried oregano

1 Tbsp fresh or dried thyme

3 garlic cloves, thinly sliced

2¼ lb [1 kg] ripe plum tomatoes, quartered

5 Tbsp purple cabbage pickle juice, or to taste (page 139)

2 dried chipotles, seeded, plus 1 Tbsp pickled jalapeños or 2 chipotles in adobo sauce

Scant 1½ cups [350 ml] water

For the tofu sour cream:

14 oz [400 g] silken tofu, drained

1 Tbsp olive oil

Juice of 1 lemon

½ tsp sea salt

For the tortillas and to assemble:

Vegetable oil, for oiling and frying

14 x 6-in [15-cm] diameter blue (or white) corn tortillas

Vegan cheese, such as Daiya Cheddar-style slices

I had something similar to this cooked by a woman chef, Pilar Cabrera from Oaxaca at Azul Condesa restaurant in Mexico City, or DF ("Dey Effe") as the locals call it. While it's a typical Oaxacan dish, it is very unusual, with a tangy flavor. The red hibiscus with the blue corn enchiladas and the pickled purple cabbage lend this dish deep sunset colors. And blue corn is the only truly blue food! It's easy to buy hibiscus flowers online and at healthfood stores.

The more unusual ingredients are readily available on Mexican food websites. I urge you to discover chipotle in adobo—just one of which can transform a sauce, a stew, or a vegan mayonnaise dish.

To make the filling, place the hibiscus flowers in a heatproof bowl, cover with boiling water and leave to steep overnight. (At the same time, prepare your purple pickled cabbage to leave overnight.)

In the morning, strain the flowers. Heat the olive oil in a large, heavy pan over medium heat, add the onion and garlic and sauté until soft. Add the hibiscus flowers, carrots, daikon, sugar, oregano, and thyme. Cook, stirring, for about 15 minutes until the carrots are soft and the liquid has evaporated. Season with salt and pepper and set aside to keep warm.

For the pickled purple cabbage, put the sugar, salt and vinegar in a small saucepan and simmer until dissolved. Let it cool, then toss with the cabbage in a bowl and leave to stand overnight. The next day, drain the cabbage, reserving the liquid.

For the chipotle tomato sauce, heat the vegetable oil in a saucepan and fry the onion until soft, then add the bay leaves, oregano, thyme, garlic, tomatoes, some salt, the pickle juice, chipotles, and water. Place over medium heat, and cook, stirring occasionally, for about 20 minutes until the tomatoes begin to fall apart. Remove from the heat and remove the bay leaves. Transfer the mixture to a blender and purée until smooth.

To make the tofu sour cream, whisk the ingredients together and store in the fridge until ready to use.

Oil a large roasting pan and preheat the oven to 350°F [180°C]. Pour enough of the tomato sauce to cover the bottom of the roasting pan.

Pour enough oil into a large skillet to reach a depth of ¾ in [2 cm]. Heat over medium-high heat. Working in batches, submerge the tortillas and cook, turning once, for 30 to 45 seconds until they soften. Drain on paper towels. (A lower-fat option is to steam the tortillas in a vegetable steamer, or microwave them in a tortilla warmer.)

To assemble, put a small amount of hibiscus filling in the center of each tortilla, plus a slice of the cheese, then roll to enclose, placing them all in the roasting pan on top of the sauce. Smother the enchiladas with more tomato sauce and bake in the oven for 10 minutes. Garnish with the tofu sour cream and pickled purple cabbage, and serve.

Smoked Basil & Beet Tofu Baked in Coconut

Serves 4 to 6

1 pack of banana leaves, cut into 12-in [30-cm] squares (1 per guest)

7 oz [200 g] basil tofu, drained and cut into ¼-in [6-mm] slices (to make your own, see page 33)

7 oz [200 g] smoked tofu, drained and cut into ¼-in [6-mm] slices

7 oz [200 g] firm tofu, dyed with 1 Tbsp beet powder rubbed in or plain, cut into ¼-in [6-mm] slices

4 to 6 small bird's eye chiles, seeded and thinly sliced

Thumb of ginger, peeled and very finely chopped

1 cup [250 ml] unsweetened coconut cream

Tamari sauce, for drizzling

Handful of cilantro leaves

I do like to cook things "en papillote"—that is, wrapped in leaves or baking parchment—as it seals in all the flavor. I specify cooking this in banana leaves, but you can use baking parchment if you like. This is a real dinner party dish. Banana leaves are cheapest if bought frozen in Asian/Chinese supermarkets.

Preheat the oven to 400°F [200°C].

First prepare the banana leaves by roasting them slightly over an open flame or dry-roasting them in a large skillet, until they soften. Don't let them burn or go black. Then lay the banana leaf squares flat and arrange the different colored slices of tofu, overlapping one another, on top.

Add a few slices of chile, a pinch of chopped ginger, 1 Tbsp coconut cream, a drizzle of tamari sauce, and a few cilantro leaves to each. Close the packages, using either kitchen string or cocktail sticks. Place them carefully in a baking pan and bake for 25 minutes.

Serve with noodles or rice and a citrus salad (see page 99).

Stuffed Yellow Zucchini & Red Peppers

Serves 4 to 6

1 whole garlic bulb

Olive oil, for roasting and frying

⅔ cup [100 g] unroasted buckwheat groats (kasha)

Scant 1 cup [200 ml] vegetable stock

5 small, round yellow zucchini

3 small Romano peppers

7 oz [200 g] cauliflower florets

7 oz [200 g] broccoli florets

4 cherry tomatoes, quartered

Couple of sprigs of thyme, leaves only

Sea salt and freshly ground black pepper

Preheat the oven to 400°F [200°C]. Toss the garlic bulb in olive oil and roast on a baking sheet for about 15 minutes or until softened. Then remove from the oven, let cool, and squeeze out the softened garlic flesh. Set aside. (You can do more of these and keep them in a little bowl in the fridge, useful for many recipes.)

Put the kasha and stock in a pan, cover and bring to a boil. Turn down to a simmer and cook until all the water is absorbed, as when cooking rice.

When I cook, I often start with color. In my mind's eye, I saw a yellow and red dish with a little bit of green, and I had some round sunflower-yellow zucchini and bright red Romano peppers in the fridge. Slice off the top of the zucchini, retaining the "hat," then hollow out the centers, making sure you don't gouge any holes in the side. Cut the stalk ends off the peppers, remove the seeds, and cut each into 3 rings. Pack the zucchini and peppers into an oiled, medium-sized baking dish, alternating the colors.

Then, do this new thing that's all the rage: make couscous from vegetables. You just put the raw cauliflower and broccoli florets into a food processor and process until they look like couscous. (You can also use this technique to make a raw salad.)

Mix the kasha and vegetable couscous with the cherry tomatoes. Heat some olive oil in a skillet, add this mixture along with the roast garlic cloves and thyme leaves, and fry for about 5 minutes, then add salt and pepper to taste.

Spoon the mixture into the zucchini and peppers, making sure you can see a little bit of red cherry tomato in the yellow zucchini stuffing. If there is any tasty oil left from the garlic clove roasting and the couscous frying, drizzle that over the zucchini and peppers. Replace the "hats" on all of them.

Cover the dish with foil and bake in the oven (still at 400°F [200°C]) for 15 to 20 minutes, removing the foil for the last 5 minutes.

Chocolate Smoky Tofu Mole in Tacos with Grilled Calçots

Serves 4 to 8

In Oaxaca, they have all kinds of *mole*, a kind of paste or thick sauce—yellow, green, red—but a chocolate *mole* is one of the most unique. This chocolate *mole* with smoked tofu is as satisfying as any meat dish. Calçots are a Catalan dish of very young leeks simply broiled, slightly blackened and dressed with olive oil. A great combo for tacos. The typically Oaxacan sauce will make double the amount you need for the tofu, so either freeze half, or if you have more guests, double the amount of tofu. You can serve this as tacos or just as a stew with rice.

2½ Tbsp olive oil

1 onion, diced

3 garlic cloves, minced

Generous 2 oz [60 g] vegan dark chocolate

8¾ oz [350 g] whole tomatoes

1 tsp ground cumin

½ tsp ground cinnamon

¼ tsp ground allspice

2 dried ancho chilies

2 dried chipotle chilies

2 Tbsp vegetable bouillon powder

1¾ cups [170 g] blanched or ground almonds

2 Tbsp strong agave nectar

14 oz [400 g] firm smoked tofu, drained and cut into 1-in [2.5-cm] cubes

1 pack of calçots, young leeks or scallions, trimmed

14 corn tortillas

Sea salt

To serve:

Slices of avocado

A fistful of alfalfa sprouts

Sprigs of cilantro

Lime wedges

Heat the oil in a pan and fry the onion and garlic until soft, then add the chocolate, tomatoes, cumin, cinnamon, and allspice. Cook slowly over medium-low heat for 15 to 20 minutes while you prepare the chilies.

Meanwhile, split all the dried chilies and discard the seeds, then briefly toast the chilies in a dry skillet until soft. Place in a 1 pint [½ L] heatproof pitcher with the vegetable bouillon powder. Fill up the pitcher with boiling water and leave to soak for 10 minutes, stirring once or twice.

Put the almonds, the chili and stock mixture, the cooked sauce, agave nectar, and 1 Tbsp salt in a powerful blender. Starting on a low speed, process together, increasing the speed as you go, until smooth. Transfer the sauce to a deep, wide skillet.

Add the tofu cubes to the sauce and poach until the tofu expands slightly and the sauce is bubbling but not boiling.

In the meantime, roast the calçots, young leeks, or scallions in a dry skillet or directly over a flame, turning them, until soft and slightly blackened around the edges (this makes them sweet).

To serve, place some of the tofu pieces and the chocolate mole in the tacos and fold so that the opening is upwards. Tuck in a leek or scallion and a few avocado slices. Top with alfalfa sprouts, the calçots, and cilantro. Season with salt and squeeze over some lime juice.

Ital Stew with Ginger Chayote & Trinidadian Green Seasoning

Serves 6

3 Tbsp coconut oil

4 scallions, chopped into 2-in [5-cm] lengths

3 garlic cloves, minced

10 allspice berries

3 carrots, peeled and finely sliced into rounds

1 ripe plantain, peeled and cut into ¾-in [2-cm] slices

14-oz [400-g] can of black-eyed peas, drained

1⅔ cups [400 ml] canned coconut milk

2 cups [480 ml] vegetable stock

19 oz [530 g] canned callaloo leaves

2 large yams (purple or yellow) or eddoes, peeled and cut into quarters or eighths (or 2¼ lb [1 kg] pumpkin, cut into thick slices)

2 sweet potatoes, peeled and cut into quarters

Kernels cut from 2 fresh corn cobs (see page 88)

3 sprigs of thyme

1 small, sturdy Scotch bonnet chile

Sea salt

Chopped cilantro, to garnish

Continuing our journey around the world, let's visit Jamaica and the Rastafarian community, where "ital" means "vital." Many words start with "i" in the Rastafarian dialect, to signify the unity of "I" or "eye" with God and nature. Rastas are mostly vegan; they try to live and eat naturally, with no processed food, sometimes no salt, using only clay or wood vessels. I made this stew for the funeral of my neighbors' father who was a Rastafarian. Authentic Caribbean funerals have nine nights of mourning, a tradition that started in Africa. On the ninth night, food and over-proofed rum are provided, and towards midnight, the spirit of the deceased is "seen." Family and friends sing, sending the spirit on its way.

You'll need some great Caribbean ingredients here. Yam has many varieties, some of which are nicer than others (I'm not keen on the slimier ones). Americans use the word "yam" interchangeably with sweet potatoes, but this is incorrect; they are quite different. Cookbook writer Catherine Phipps, who spent a few months in the Caribbean, says the only way to buy a genuine Scotch bonnet is to smell it. She digs her thumbnail in to get at the flesh (hoping the shop assistant won't notice!) and if it smells floral, it's genuine. Chayote is also known as cho-cho or christophine. I've seen all these ingredients in big supermarkets and ethnic stores.

I hope you all "overstand" this recipe, as Rastas would say! ("Understand" is considered rather negative.) The Ginger Chayote and Trinidadian Green Seasoning are both on page 146, and brilliant dishes in themselves.

Heat the coconut oil in a large, heavy-bottomed saucepan, add the scallions and garlic and fry until soft, then add the allspice berries, carrots, and plantain. Stir, then add the black-eyed peas. Continue to cook over low heat for 10 minutes, then add the coconut milk and vegetable stock, followed by the callaloo, yams or eddoes, sweet potatoes, corn kernels and thyme.

Add salt to taste and cook over low heat for about 30 to 40 minutes, or until the potatoes and yams are soft enough to pierce with a fork. Fifteen minutes before the end of cooking, add the whole Scotch bonnet. Check the seasoning before serving, garnished with cilantro. Accompany with Ginger Chayote and Trinidadian Green Seasoning (see page 146).

Ginger Chayote

Serves 4

2 chayote, thinly
  sliced

2 to 3 Tbsp coconut oil

2-in [5-cm] piece of
  ginger, peeled and
  julienned

2 garlic cloves, minced

1 sprig of thyme

3 to 5 scallions,
  chopped into 2-in
  [5-cm] lengths

1 not-too-ripe pear,
  cored and thinly
  sliced (optional)

Sea salt

Chayote, cho-chos, or christophines look a bit like pears and have a subtle flavor, between a melon and a cucumber, with a crisp texture. You'll find them in ethnic stores and they are one of the more popular Caribbean vegetables, but they are also used in Asian and Mexican cooking.

Parboil the chayote slices for 5 minutes in boiling, salted water, then drain. Heat the coconut oil in a heavy-bottomed skillet and fry the chayote slices with the ginger, garlic and thyme. Add the scallions with the pear, if using, and season with salt.

Trinidadian Green Seasoning

3 whole garlic bulbs, roasted
  (see page 141)

Bunch of thyme, leaves only

Bunch of cilantro, leaves only

Handful of basil, leaves only

Bunch of chives

3 sprigs of oregano, leaves only

1 celery stalk, roughly chopped

Handful of parsley, leaves only

2 green chiles, seeded if you
  don't want too much heat

5 scallions, roughly chopped

1 green bell pepper, seeded

Bunch of chadon beni (Mexican
  cilantro), leaves only
  (optional)

Juice of 1 lemon

1½ Tbsp sea salt, or to taste

This green seasoning became a favorite condiment of mine over the course of writing this book; it is equally good on toast, or with fries. Chadon beni can be bought in Chinese stores as "sawtooth" or "long cilantro", and it has a very strong fresh cilantro flavor.

Put all the ingredients into a food processor and pulverize to a paste.

Zucchini Blossoms with Mint & Apple Salad

Serves 4

For the apple salad:

3 Tbsp cider vinegar

½ tsp brown sugar

1 tsp sea salt

2 crisp apples, cored and thinly sliced

For the flowers:

5¼ oz [150 g] Smoky Chipotle Cashew Cheese (see page 33) or 8 Tbsp shredded Daiya Cheddar-style block vegan cheese

Handful of mint leaves, finely chopped, plus extra leaves to garnish

8 zucchini blossoms

Vegetable oil, for deep-frying

Maple syrup, for drizzling

For the batter:

Scant 1 cup [200 ml] cold sparkling water

1½ cups [200 g] tempura flour OR scant 1¼ cups [160 g] all-purpose flour sifted with ⅓ cup [40g] cornstarch

1 tsp sea salt

Edible flowers are a somewhat neglected part of the plant-based diet. With this recipe, you literally can't go wrong. People will be so impressed.

▾▪▪▪▪▪▪▪▪◢▪▪▪▪▪▪▪▪▪▪▪▪▪▪▪▪▪▪▪▪▪▪▪▪▪▪▪▪▪

Prepare the apple salad by mixing the vinegar, sugar, and salt together in a bowl. Then toss in the apple slices and chill in the fridge for an hour.

Mix the cheese and the mint together, then carefully unfurl the flowers (check for insects) and stuff a walnut-sized ball of stuffing inside each flower. Reshape the flowers to enclose the stuffing securely.

To make the batter, add the sparkling water to the flour and salt. Do not over-stir. Lumps are fine; they add interest.

Pour enough oil into a deep pan to deep-fry the zucchini blossoms. This is best done in a proper deep-fat fryer, or in a saucepan with tongs and paper towels to drain them on. Zucchini blossoms are expensive and delicate, so you don't want them to move about too much. They must be in oil just deep enough to cover them. Heat the oil to 350°F [180°C]. Dip the zucchini blossoms into the thick batter, then carefully add to the hot oil and deep-fry until pale golden.

Remove to a plate and drizzle some maple syrup on top. Serve with a small portion of the apple salad and some mint leaves.

Watermelon Stir-Fry with Rice

Serves 4

3 Tbsp sesame oil

3 garlic cloves, minced

1-in [2.5-cm] piece of ginger, peeled and cut into fine strips

1 red onion, halved and sliced

2 tsp soy sauce

2 Tbsp hoisin sauce

1 tsp sea salt

½ tsp freshly ground black pepper

1½ small handfuls [100 g] snow peas

1 cup [100 g] baby corn cobs

About 2½ cups [400 g] watermelon flesh, skin and rind removed (see note below), cut into $^3/_8$-inch [1-cm] thick wedges

1 Tbsp sweet chili sauce

Cilantro leaves, to garnish

Rice, to serve

Note:
Do not discard the rind of the watermelon—the white part between the red and the green skin—as it can be used to make pickles, southern Dolly-Parton style (see page 24). Or you could toss the rind in, separately, at the beginning; it is a little like cooked marrow squash.

Despite exhortations from the great and the good to be a "locavore," sourcing fruit and veg locally, I must admit to a recent obsession with the tropics. Take watermelons, for instance. They're almost camp as a fruit, the outsize prehistoric green bowling ball with its juicy pink interior studded with black seeds. No artist can resist painting them. But they are a pain in the bicep to shop for... you need serious muscles to carry them, or have them delivered.

This is an unusual use of watermelon, but I do like the contrast of sweet, crisp red flesh with savory Chinese flavors. Other uses for any leftover watermelon flesh include freezing and blitzing it to make the best watermelon cocktails.

Heat the sesame oil in a wok or a heavy-bottomed saucepan and throw in the garlic, ginger, and onion. Fry for 5 minutes or so, then add the soy sauce, hoisin sauce, salt, pepper, snow peas, baby corn cobs, watermelon, and sweet chili sauce. Fry over high heat, moving the ingredients around rapidly but carefully with a wooden spoon.

Garnish with cilantro leaves and serve with rice.

Cornbread & Gravy with Portobello Steaks

Serves 4

For the cornbread:

Scant ¾ cup [175 ml] unsweetened soy milk

2 Tbsp cider vinegar

1 tsp egg replacer

1 Tbsp water

Heaping 1⅛ cups [175 g] cornmeal or polenta

¾ cup [100 g] all-purpose flour

¼ cup [50 g] brown sugar

1 tsp baking soda

1 tsp sea salt

3 Tbsp vegetable oil, plus extra for oiling

Kernels cut from 2 fresh corn cobs (optional) (see page 88)

For the mushrooms:

2 Tbsp vegan margarine

2 garlic cloves, minced

Handful of flat-leaf parsley, finely chopped

Pinch of sea salt

4 large portobello mushrooms

Freshly ground black pepper

For the gravy:

1 cup [20 g] dried mushrooms

1 Tbsp vegetable bouillon powder

Scant 2½ Tbsp [35 ml] olive oil

2 shallots, finely chopped

2 garlic cloves, minced

1 cup [100 g] fresh mushrooms, thinly sliced

2 Tbsp dark soy sauce (or Bragg Liquid Aminos or Maggi Liquid Seasoning)

½ cup [125 ml] vegan red wine

3 Tbsp all-purpose flour

Freshly ground black pepper

I love cornbread. In this one I've added fresh corn for extra texture. Serve with gravy and grilled portobello mushrooms.

Preheat the oven to 400°F [200°C].

Create the buttermilk equivalent by combining the soy milk and cider vinegar and letting sit for 10 minutes.

Combine the egg replacer with the water, then mix all the cornbread ingredients together. It will be quite liquid. For chunkier cornbread, include the corn kernels. Pour the mixture into an oiled ovenproof cast-iron skillet and bake in the oven for 30 to 40 minutes until golden and a skewer inserted into the center comes out clean.

For the mushrooms, mix together the vegan margarine, garlic, parsley, salt, and plenty of pepper, and cover the brown gills of each mushroom with it.

For the gravy, put the dried mushrooms and bouillon powder in a ½-qt [½-L] heatproof pitcher and fill with boiling water. Set aside to soak for 30 minutes.

Heat the oil in a medium saucepan over medium-high heat, add the shallots and cook until softened, then add the garlic and the fresh mushrooms. Add the soy sauce and red wine and cook until hot but not boiling, then stir in the flour very rapidly. Add the dried mushrooms and most of the soaking stock, and season with black pepper. Keep the gravy on a low simmer, adding more soaking stock if it gets too thick. (This gravy is great on virtually anything, including mashed potatoes.)

Preheat the broiler to hot and broil the portobello mushrooms until they are hot all the way through and the garlic mixture is bubbling. Serve with hunks of cornbread and the gravy.

Jamaican Rice & Peas with Fresh Coconut

Serves 6

1¼ cups [200 g] dried black-eyed peas, pinto, or black turtle beans

½ onion, peeled

2 garlic cloves, peeled—1 whole and 1 sliced

4 to 6 allspice berries

2 scallions, finely sliced

½ red bell pepper, seeded and sliced

Scant 2 to 3 oz [50 to 75 g] creamed coconut

2 to 3 fresh sprigs or 1 Tbsp dried thyme

1 Tbsp soy sauce

1 Scotch bonnet chile

½ fresh coconut, peeled and sliced (see page 18)

2 small slices of fresh ginger

Scant 3 cups [500 g] basmati rice

1 Tbsp coconut oil

Sea salt and freshly ground black pepper

My neighbour Karen, also a single mom, who comes from a Jamaican background, has started a sideline in selling proper Jamaican food to other moms outside the school gate. She's named herself Msricenpeas. Parents are flocking to buy tubs of her rice and peas, callaloo, and jerk chicken. I can't blame them—it's delicious, healthy, and while seemingly simple, it's time-consuming to make properly.

Rice and peas is the mainstay food of Jamaican cuisine. "Peas" are beans, and the further south, the darker the legume. Caribbean islands near to the American South will often use the black-eyed pea as I have. Jamaicans use the pinto bean. Islands closer to South America will use the small black turtle bean. The smaller the pea, the sweeter it is.

Karen kindly gave me her recipe. A couple of pointers: it surprised me that she soaked the peas with garlic and onion "to soften them." Softening those peas is important. And I had some fresh coconut, so I cooked my peas with a few large slices. It lent a rich depth to the flavor.

Soak the beans in filtered or cooled boiled water from the kettle, overnight if possible, adding the onion and whole garlic clove halfway through (yes, I have woken up in the middle of the night to put onion and garlic in my beans). Drain, discard the onion and garlic and transfer the beans to a heavy pot or casserole dish.

Add the allspice berries and sliced garlic and cover everything with boiling water. Simmer over low heat for 45 minutes, then add the scallions and red pepper and simmer until the beans are cooked. Don't let them get too soft; they should smell sweet and creamy.

Pour just enough hot water over the creamed coconut to dissolve, then add to the beans. You can add more or less if you prefer; I find too much coconut cream makes the rice greasy. Add the thyme, soy sauce, whole Scotch bonnet, fresh coconut, and ginger and simmer, covered, for 15 minutes. Then fish out and discard the whole Scotch bonnet. Wash the rice, and once it is free of starch, add it to the beans and stir with a fork. Add about 4½ cups [1 L] water and the coconut oil. Add salt and pepper to taste and cook, covered, over low heat (or in the oven at 325°F [160°C] until the rice is soft and fluffy, checking on the water levels, but without stirring. Enjoy!

Wild Mushroom Forest Pie

Serves 6 to 8

For the pastry:

3¾ cups [500 g] all-purpose flour

1 tsp sea salt

⅔ cup [150 ml] olive oil, semi-frozen (see recipe introduction)

¼ to ⅓ cup [60 to 80 ml] ice water

1 Tbsp cider vinegar

For the mushroom filling:

Scant 3 Tbsp [40 ml] olive oil

3 shallots, minced

2 garlic cloves, minced

Scant 1¾ lb [750 g] wild mushrooms

Scant ½ cup [100 ml] soy cream

⅞ cup [200 ml] vermouth or vegan white wine

12 stemmed mushrooms for decoration, e.g., enoki

Vegan margarine, melted, for brushing

Unsweetened almond or soy milk, to glaze

Sea salt and freshly ground black pepper

In the US, Isa Chandra Moskowitz and Terry Hope Romero are THE vegan cookbook authors. They've known each other for 20 years, meeting on the New York punk scene. I asked Terry if I could nick her recipe for vegan pie crust. It's really quite ingenious. Rather than using butter or shortening, use partially frozen olive oil. Just freeze in a plastic container for a couple of hours before using it.

To make the pastry, sift the flour and salt into a large bowl. Working quickly so that it stays cold, add the olive oil by the tablespoonful, cutting it into the flour with your fingers or a pastry cutter, until the mixture appears pebbly. Mix ¼ cup [60 ml] ice water with the vinegar and drizzle 2 Tbsp into the flour. Stir into the dough, adding more liquid 1 Tbsp at a time until it holds together to form a soft ball; you may not need all of the ice water. Take care not to overwork the dough. (You can make the pastry in a food processor if you prefer.)

Divide the dough in half and roll into balls, then press each into a flat disc. Wrap each in plastic wrap and leave to rest in the fridge for 30 minutes.

Heat the olive oil for the filling in a skillet over medium heat, add the shallots and garlic and sweat for 20 minutes, or until soft. Add the mushrooms, soy cream, and vermouth or wine and cook until thick. Season and set aside to cool. Meanwhile, preheat the oven to 400°F [200°C].

Roll out both discs of pastry to ⅛ in [3 mm], to fit the bottom and top of your pie dish (approximately 8 by 8 in [20 by 20 cm]. Fit the bottom crust into the pie dish, add the cooled filling and gently press down to get everything in. Cover with the top crust, pinch the edges together to seal, trim any excess dough, and crimp the edges with the tines of a fork. Make 5 slits in the top of the pie and poke the stemmed mushroom into them (the holes also help steam escape). Brush the top of the mushrooms with a little vegan margarine, and brush the pie with the milk.

Cover the pie with foil and bake for 20 minutes. Reduce the oven temperature to 350°F [180°C] and bake for 30 minutes more, or until the filling bubbles up through the edges, removing the foil for the last 15 minutes so that the top will go golden.

Nut Roast

Serves 8 to 10

This dish has such a bad reputation I almost feared to tackle it. It sums up every cliché about vegetarian or vegan food: brown, wholesome, heavy. But you'll find that despite its worthy appearance, this recipe has a stalwart fan club, even amongst meat eaters. Sandwiched inside the basic nut roast in my recipe, there are two alternative fillings: one with traditional Christmassy vegetables and another with a spicier Malaysian feel if you want something a little different.

For the filling: 2 alternatives

Filling 1: (traditional Christmas dinner):

7 oz [200 g] parsnips, peeled and halved lengthwise

7 oz [200 g] Jerusalem artichokes, peeled and halved

Scant ½ cup [100 ml] olive oil

Several sprigs of rosemary

1 Tbsp ground cumin

2 Tbsp sea salt

Preheat the oven to 400°F [200°C].

Put the parsnips and artichokes into a baking dish and pour the olive oil over them, tossing them with your hands so that they are well covered. Snip some rosemary leaves over and sprinkle over the cumin, then the sea salt. Roast in the oven for 35 minutes until golden.

Filling 2:

2 red bell peppers, seeded and cut into thin strips

6 tomatoes, diced

⅓ cup [75ml] olive oil

1 dried red chili

½ fresh coconut, peeled and ground in a food processor or finely chopped (see page 18)

Sea salt

Fry the peppers and tomatoes together in the oil until the peppers are soft. Crumble over the dried chili, taking care not to add the seeds if you don't want it too hot. Add the finely chopped coconut, and salt to taste, and fry for a few minutes.

For the nut roast:

Generous 3 Tbsp [50 ml] olive oil, for frying and oiling

4 shallots or 2 onions, diced

Cloves of 1 whole garlic bulb, minced

14 oz [400 g] cashew nuts or 7 oz [200 g] cashews and 7 oz [200 g] macadamia nuts

10½ oz [300 g] sourdough bread crumbs (for a gluten-free version, start with 1½ cups [300 g] uncooked brown rice, cook and cool)

⅞ cup [200 ml] vegetable stock

Juice of ½ lemon

½ cup [50 g] almonds or pecans

Sea salt and freshly ground black pepper

Fresh herbs, to garnish

Heat some olive oil in a skillet over medium heat and add the shallots or onions with the garlic. Soften until translucent and sweet.

Preheat the oven to 400°F [200°C].

Grind the cashew and macadamia nuts in a blender, food processor, or by hand, leaving some whole to add interest to the texture, if you like. Mix together the ground nuts, bread crumbs (or brown rice), fried shallot or onion and garlic mixture, the vegetable stock, lemon juice, and salt and pepper to taste.

Oil a 9-by-5-in [1-kg] loaf pan and line with baking parchment. Neatly place the almonds or pecan nuts all over the bottom—when the nut roast is turned out, they will be the decoration on top. Put half the nut roast mixture into the pan. Top with one of the filling options. If using the parsnips and artichokes, then lay the parsnips lengthwise along the loaf pan, dotted with the artichokes. If using the pepper, tomato, and coconut filling, just spread it on top.

Add the rest of the nut roast mixture over the filling, cover with foil, and bake for 30 minutes. Remove the foil and bake for another 10 minutes until the top is dark golden. Leave to cool in the pan for 30 minutes.

Turn the loaf out onto a decorative plate. Garnish with fresh herbs and serve by the slice.

Spectacular Russian Stuffed Cabbage Rose

Serves 4

A recipe adapted from *A Taste of Russia* (by Darra Goldstein): whole stuffed baked cabbage. As the original was stuffed with meat, I made up my own filling. It looks terribly pretty unfurled as you stuff the filling inside each leaf. And later, once cooked, it resembles a Christmas pudding, so it makes a festive vegan centerpiece. You can also do this with mini cabbages, one per person, in which case adjust the recipe accordingly.

• •

1 Savoy cabbage

Heaping 1⅛ cups [200 g] red quinoa

Generous 3 Tbsp [50 ml] olive oil, plus extra for brushing and oiling

2 white onions, finely diced

1 cup [100 g] wild or brown mushrooms, chopped

1 tsp ground cumin

3½ oz [100 g] fresh dill, plus extra to garnish

10½ oz [300 g] frozen cranberries, plus extra to garnish

3 Tbsp sugar

1¼ cups [300 ml] soy cream

Sea salt and freshly ground black pepper

Boil or steam the cabbage by plunging it whole into boiling, salted water in a large saucepan. Cook for around 15 minutes or until still firm, but tender. Remove from the pan and leave to cool.

Preheat the oven to 350°F [180°C].

Rinse the quinoa in a strainer until the water runs clear. Use double the volume of water to quinoa—in this case 2¼ cups [540 ml] water—and put both in a medium saucepan with 1 tsp salt. Bring to a boil, then cook for about 20 minutes. Leave to stand for 5 minutes off the heat and with the lid on. Then uncover and fluff it up with a fork.

Heat the olive oil in a pan, add the onions, and cook until softened, then add the mushrooms, cumin, dill, and salt and pepper to taste. Add a third of the cranberries and 1 Tbsp of the sugar and cook until they break down. Mix the drained quinoa with the cranberry mixture. Take your cooled cabbage and carefully open out the leaves (it looks like a flower when you serve it).

Brush all the leaves with olive oil seasoned with salt and pepper. Using a tablespoon, pack a spoonful of mixture into the base of each leaf. When finished, pull all the leaves up and close the cabbage. Tie to secure with kitchen string and place in an oiled baking pan. Brush the top of the cabbage with oil and bake for 30 minutes, then remove from the oven and cover the cabbage with the soy cream. Return it to the oven and bake for another 10 to 15 minutes.

Meanwhile, put the rest of the cranberries and sugar in a saucepan over medium-high heat. Cook until the sugar has dissolved and the berries start to go mushy.

Place the baked cabbage whole on a serving platter and snip off the string. Garnish with extra cranberries and some dill. It can then be sliced like a cake.

Roast Parsnips & Jerusalem Artichokes

Serves 4 to 6

Sugar-sweet roast
veg with added
cumin to combat
flatulence, which
might help with
the "fartichokes."
I can't guarantee
it, though.

3¼ lb [1.5 kg] parsnips, peeled and trimmed

2¼ lb [1 kg] Jerusalem artichokes, peeled

⅓ cup [75 ml] olive oil

1 Tbsp sea salt

1 tsp cumin seeds

Freshly ground black pepper

Preheat the oven to 375°F [190°C]. Place the parsnips
and artichokes in a roasting pan and toss them in
the olive oil and salt. Bake for 45 minutes or until
golden. Add the cumin and some black pepper.

Eggplant Baked with Miso Glaze

Serves 4

Serve this simple entrée or
side from Japan, known as
nasu dengaku, with sushi
rice or noodles, the green
bean dish (see page 121) and
some pickles. Miso is a very
healthy fermented foodstuff;
some even claim that it
combats radiation sickness.

2 Tbsp mirin

2 Tbsp sake or rice wine

4 Tbsp white miso

2 Tbsp brown sugar

2 large, shiny, firm
eggplants

4 tsp sesame oil

For the garnish:

Toasted sesame seeds

Scallions, green part
only, cut into lengths
of 1½ in [4 cm]

Preheat the oven to 375°F [190°C].

Place the mirin and sake or rice wine
in a small saucepan and bring to a
simmer over medium heat. Simmer for
about 2 minutes, then add the miso and
stir until smooth. Stir in the sugar
and reduce the heat to very low.

Cut the eggplants in half lengthwise.
Score the flesh side of each eggplant
half with a crisscross diamond pattern
and brush with the sesame oil. Place,
cut side down, on a baking sheet and
bake in the oven for 10 minutes.

Heat the broiler to very hot. Turn the
eggplants over and place under the hot
broiler for about 5 minutes. You want
them just light brown, soft inside and
slightly crispy on top.

Spoon the miso sauce onto the cut sides
and put them back under the broiler for
another minute until the sauce bubbles.
Sprinkle with toasted sesame seeds and
scallions and serve.

Roast Potatoes in Coconut Oil

Serves 4

Coconut oil has a high smoking point, which means that you get crispy, fluffy roast potatoes every time. There is a rule about roast potatoes—people will always want more and there are never enough. So do more than you think is necessary. And don't hold back on the fat and salt.

▼▪▪▪▪▪▪▪▪▪▪▪▪▪▪▪▪▪▪▪▪▪

4½ lb [2 kg] floury potatoes, peeled and cut into quarters or similar sizes

3 Tbsp coconut oil

Generous 3 Tbsp [50 ml] olive oil

Sea salt

Preheat the oven to 400°F [200°C]. Parboil the potatoes for 10 minutes in a large saucepan of boiling, salted water. Drain and transfer to a roasting pan, shaking the potatoes to rough them up a bit.

Add the coconut oil, olive oil, and salt to taste. Turn to coat the potatoes, then bake for 45 minutes, or until golden and crispy, giving the pan a shake halfway through the cooking time.

Variations:

Originally, potatoes were from the New World, specifically the Peruvian Andes. So I've come up with some interesting flavor combinations (which can be applied to most roast vegetables) to liven up the Sunday roast or Christmas dinner.

Tropical: Roast slices of blood orange with the potatoes. Add fresh coconut, cut into ¼-in [6-mm] strips, just before the end as it cooks more quickly. Garnish with cilantro pesto or dried red pepper flakes.

Italian: My Italian great-grandmother Nanny Savino taught this recipe to my very British mother. Pour a can of tomatoes onto the potatoes and mix it in. Add a few cloves of garlic, and crumble some oregano onto it.

Middle Eastern: Add garlic, sumac, harissa, cumin, and coriander seeds to the potatoes.

Saffron: Add a large pinch of saffron strands to the parboiling water.

Wilted Day Lilies with Mustard Greens

Serves 4

2 to 3 Tbsp olive oil

2¼ lb [1 kg] mustard greens or other dark greens, washed, stems cut off if they are thick

2 garlic cloves, minced

1 red chile, seeded and finely sliced

8 to 10 day lilies, stamens removed

Sea salt

Steamed rice or boiled tapioca, to serve

Day lilies are incredibly sweet, like honey. Pick unsprayed ones once they have opened for those brief few hours. Remove the stamens and make sure there are no insects.

Heat the oil in a large skillet over medium-high heat. Add the mustard or other greens, garlic, and chile, with sea salt to taste. After 5 or so minutes when the greens are wilted, add the day lilies on top and let them wilt also.

Serve the lilies hot with steamed rice or boiled tapioca.

Artichoke, Potato, Spinach, & Tofu B'stilla with Poppy Seeds & Rose Petals

Serves 6 to 8

One of the most stunning meals I've ever had was at a Moroccan restaurant in LA. We were served vast platters with pyramids of couscous and a b'stilla, an exotic filled pastry pie. Try this easy vegan b'stilla, an explosion of sweet and savory.

2 large potatoes, peeled

Olive oil, for frying, oiling, and brushing

1 onion, sliced

2 garlic cloves, sliced

1 cinnamon stick

18 oz [500 g] fresh spinach

14 oz [400 g] firm tofu, drained and cut into 1-in [2.5-cm] squares

14 oz [400 g] canned artichoke hearts, drained and halved

½ cup [50 g] slivered almonds

2 Tbsp [30 g] green raisins (available from Indian stores)

1 Tbsp sugar

Heaping 2 Tbsp [20 g] pine nuts

1 Tbsp ras el hanout spice mix

1 tsp harissa

1 to 2 preserved lemons, cut into small pieces

Handful of black olives, pitted

4 large sheets of phyllo pastry

Poppy seeds, for sprinkling

Powdered sugar

Sea salt

Rose petals, to garnish

Boil the potatoes in a medium saucepan, with 1 tsp salt, for 15 to 20 minutes until just about tender. Drain and cut into 1-in [2.5-cm] chunks.

Heat some olive oil in a large saucepan over medium heat, add the onion and cook until soft. Add the garlic, cinnamon stick, potatoes, 1 Tbsp sea salt, and the spinach. Let the spinach cook down, then add the tofu. Add the artichoke hearts, almonds, green raisins, sugar, pine nuts, ras el hanout, and harissa. Finally, add the preserved lemons and olives. Remove the pan from the heat and let it cool.

Preheat the oven to 400°F [200°C]. To make the b'stilla, remove the base from a deep, 7-in [18-cm] springform cake pan (you need just the sides/ring as a support) and place on an oiled baking sheet. Working with one piece of phyllo at a time and keeping the rest covered with a damp dish towel, to prevent them from drying out, brush the sheet with olive oil and place it in the center of the pan, draping it over the sides. Then brush a second piece of phyllo and lay it on top, at an angle to the first. Do this with all 4 sheets until the base and pan sides are completely covered with the pastry, with the excess overhanging the sides.

Put the cooled filling mixture in the middle and fold over the overhanging phyllo to cover the top. Brush the top with olive oil and sprinkle with poppy seeds. Cover with foil and put the baking sheet, with the pan sides/ring, into the oven. Bake for 30 minutes, removing the foil after 25 minutes to let the top get crisp.

Remove from the oven, remove the springform sides/ring and transfer the b'stilla to a serving plate, using a spatula. Dust the top with powdered sugar and sprinkle with rose petals and some more black poppy seeds.

Dessert

In some ways, dessert,
so often about dairy and
eggs, is the hardest course
for the plant-based diet.
But amazing desserts can
be achieved using vegan-
friendly ingredients.

Black & Green Cheesecake
with Bengali Lime & Avocado

Serves 6 to 8

Oil spray, for greasing

For the crust:

1¼ cups [150 g] Oreo
cookies, finely ground

3 Tbsp coconut milk

For the filling:

1¼ cups [150 g] cashew nuts,
soaked in water for 2 to
4 hours, then drained

2 small avocados, peeled
and pitted

½ tsp sea salt

1 tsp vanilla paste or
1 vanilla bean, split
lengthwise

Scant ½ cup [100 ml] agave
nectar

Juice of 2 lemons

Scant ½ cup [100 ml] coconut
oil

Juice of 5 limes, plus the
pared zest of 1 for the
top (optional)

Slices of kiwi fruit,
for the top (optional)

Key limes or Mexican limes used in Key
lime pie are very different from the usual
"Persian" limes that we usually see. Key
limes are smaller, more acidic, and the flesh
is yellow. Once dried into black lime, they
are a useful ingredient in Middle Eastern
cookery. The strange thing about both Key
limes and Persian limes is that they are
ripe when the flesh is yellow, not green.

As it's sometimes hard to get hold of Key
limes, I use normal limes. But if you can
get hold of Bengali limes (I buy them at
Asian supermarkets), then do. They are
perfumed, floral, and exotic.

Lightly spray a 7-in [18-cm] loose-
bottomed cake pan with oil.

In a mixing bowl, combine the ground
Oreos and coconut milk. Press the
mixture into the bottom of the cake
pan. Chill in the fridge for about
30 minutes.

Put all the ingredients except the lime
zest and kiwi fruit into a powerful
blender. Process until smooth. Then
take the cheesecake base from the
fridge and ladle in the green filling.

Decorate with curls of pared lime
zest, or with overlapping layers of
kiwi fruit slices, or both. Chill in
the fridge for 2 hours before serving.

Chocolate, Orange, Chestnut, & Tofu Mousse with Coconut Yogurt & Marinated Blood Oranges

Serves 4

1 blood orange

2 Tbsp Cointreau

5¼ oz [150 g] vegan orange dark or dark chocolate, broken into pieces

10½ oz [300 g] very soft silken tofu, at room temperature

1¼ cups [250 g] canned sweetened crème de marrons (chestnut purée)

Glug of Cointreau or Triple Sec liqueur (optional)

Natural coconut milk yogurt (e.g., CoYo), to serve

This is just as rich and velvety as a dairy chocolate mousse, and frankly, easier to make. If you don't have blood oranges, use normal ones.

Pare a couple of strips of zest off the orange and set aside for later. Then completely peel the orange and cut a small slice from the bottom and top of the orange so that it sits on a board. Using a sharp, flexible knife, carefully remove the white pith, cutting from top to bottom around the orange and trying to retain the shape of the orange. Turn the orange on its side and cut into thin rounds. Put into a bowl, add the Cointreau and leave for a few hours.

Melt the chocolate in the microwave on full power in 30-second bursts. Do not do it for longer bursts or it will ruin (or "seize") the chocolate. Good chocolate is expensive.

Put the melted chocolate in a powerful blender with the tofu and crème de marrons and blend until smooth. Add a shot of Cointreau or Triple Sec if you wish.

Divide the mousse between 4 serving glasses or ramekins and refrigerate for 2 hours. Decorate the top with a slice or two of the marinated blood orange, the pared zest, and some coconut milk yogurt.

Rhubarb Crumble with Custard

Serves 6 to 8

2¼ lb [1 kg] rhubarb, cut
into 2-in [5-cm] lengths

½ cup [100 g] superfine
sugar

1 tsp ground ginger

½ tsp ground cinnamon

½ tsp ground nutmeg

For the crumble:

1 cup [100 g] rolled oats

¾ cup [100 g] all-purpose
flour

½ cup [100 g] brown sugar

1 tsp ground cinnamon

½ tsp sea salt

¼ cup [50 g] coconut oil

The perfect winter dessert, a British classic.

Preheat the oven to 350°F [180°C]. Oil an ovenproof dish, 11 by 7 in [28 by 18 cm].

Mix together the rhubarb, superfine sugar, ginger, cinnamon, and nutmeg and transfer to the prepared dish. Cover with foil and bake for 15 minutes. Remove from the oven and set aside.

In a bowl, combine the oats, flour, brown sugar, cinnamon, and salt. Then, with cool hands, rub the coconut oil into this mixture until it resembles bread crumbs.

Remove the foil from the rhubarb dish and sprinkle the crumble over the rhubarb. Bake for 30 to 40 minutes or until golden. Serve hot with the custard below.

Custard

Serves 6 to 8

2 Tbsp potato starch

2 Tbsp cornstarch

3¼ cups [800 ml] rice
or nut milk

½ cup [100 g] sugar

2 vanilla beans, split
lengthwise and seeds
scraped out, or
2 tsp vanilla paste

This works and tastes pretty good. It does also work with soy milk, but I prefer the flavor of rice or nut milk.

Put the potato starch and cornstarch into a saucepan and add a little of the milk, stirring to make a paste.

Warm the remaining milk in a heavy-bottomed saucepan over low heat, whisking in the sugar and vanilla seeds or paste until the sugar has dissolved. Stir with a wooden spoon for at least 5 minutes or until the custard becomes slightly transparent. It's important to cook out the starchy flavor of the flour.

Once you can run your finger down the wooden spoon and see the wood, take the custard off the heat and serve.

Roast Peaches with Lavender & Coconut Salted Caramel

Serves 4 to 6

6 ripe peaches, halved and pitted

Lavender sugar, for sprinkling

Lavender flowers, to decorate (optional)

For the coconut salted caramel:

1⅔ cups [400 ml] canned coconut milk

¼ cup [50 g] brown sugar

Pinch of good-quality sea salt, such as fleur de sel or Maldon

Choose ripe, in-season peaches for this.

To make the coconut salted caramel, heat the coconut milk and sugar in a wide-bottomed saucepan over very low heat for an hour or so until it caramelizes and thickens. Stir occasionally. Then transfer to a pitcher, adding a little sea salt. Meanwhile, preheat the oven to 350°F [180°C].

Place the peach halves cut side up in a roasting pan and sprinkle with lavender sugar. Roast for 30 minutes.

Scoop a couple of tablespoons of the salted caramel into each bowl, then top with 2 to 3 roasted peach halves. Garnish with a few fresh lavender flowers, if you like.

Chia Seed, Rose, & Raspberry Falooda

Serves 4

4 Tbsp chia seeds

1⅔ cups [400 ml] sweetened almond or rice milk, chilled

4 Tbsp superfine or coconut sugar

8 scoops of vegan vanilla ice cream

3 cups [400 g] raspberries

4 tsp rosewater

Mint leaves, to garnish

This is an Indian "sundae" traditionally made with basil seeds, which expand and have a soft gelatinous texture with a nutty center. A falooda can alternatively be made with vermicelli, which is something most Westerners are not too keen on—it's like rice pudding, but with pasta. So I've eliminated the vermicelli. Chia seeds are a healthy update, for chia lowers cholesterol and adds fiber to the diet.

Soak the chia seeds in the milk and sugar for at least 15 minutes.

Divide the mixture between 4 tall glasses, then add a scoop of ice cream, a few raspberries, 1 tsp rosewater, another scoop of ice cream, and more raspberries. Finally, top with a few mint leaves.

Vegan Brownies with Cinnamon or Kahlúa Cream

Serves 10

2 Tbsp ground flaxseed (golden linseed)

2 cups [250 g] all-purpose flour

⅔ cup [60 g] cocoa powder

1½ cups [300 g] superfine sugar

½ cup [100 g] cinnamon sugar

½ tsp baking powder

1 tsp good-quality sea salt, ideally fleur de sel (this gives it a lovely flavor)

½ cup [120 ml] water

Scant ½ cup [100 ml] sweetened almond or hazelnut milk

Scant 1¼ cups [280 ml] canola or peanut oil, plus extra for oiling (optional)

1 Tbsp vanilla extract or 1 Mexican vanilla bean, ground

1 Tbsp chipotle paste

1 tsp smoked paprika

3½ oz [100 g] vegan orange dark chocolate, chopped (e.g., Lindt or 2Beans)

1¾ cups [170 g] pecans

To serve:

Soy cream

Sprinkling of ground cinnamon or Kahlúa

These are fudgy, light and addictive. Even non-brownie lovers love them. I got the basic recipe from Ms. Cupcake, a London-based vegan bakery, but I've gone further by Mexicanizing them and making them richer.

Preheat the oven to 350°F [180°C]. Oil a baking pan, 13 by 9 in [33 by 23 cm], or line with baking parchment.

In a cup, whisk the flaxseed with 2 Tbsp lukewarm water and leave to soak. In a large bowl or stand mixer, combine the flour, cocoa, superfine sugar, cinnamon sugar, baking powder, and salt. Then add the water, nut milk, oil, vanilla, chipotle paste, smoked paprika, orange chocolate, the flaxseed mixture, and half the pecans.

Mix well, then pour into the prepared pan. Arrange the remaining pecans on top of the brownie mixture and bake in the oven for 20 minutes. The brownie may not look baked when it comes out, but it sets as it cools. You want a soft gooey inside. Leave in the pan to cool, then cut into bars. Serve with soy cream sprinkled with cinnamon or streaked through with a swig of Kahlúa.

No one will know they are vegan. Shh!

Passion Fruit & Rose Water Pavlova!

Serves 4 to 6

For the meringue:

3½ oz [100 g] egg replacer

1 cup [250 ml] water

1 cup [125 g] powdered
sugar

1 Tbsp rose water

For the topping:

2 generous cups [500 ml]
passion fruit juice

1 cup [200 g] superfine
sugar

4 ripe passion fruit
(they should be wrinkly)

2 quantities Coconut
Whipped Cream (see page
30) or Soyatoo Soy Whip,
whipped

I was amazed how well egg replacers work
to create something that I thought was
intrinsically about egg whites. Try it.

Preheat the oven to 225°F [110°C]. Whisk
the egg replacer with the water in a
stand mixer at top speed, or in a bowl
using an electric beater, for at least
5 minutes until soft peaks form. Then
slowly add the powdered sugar, whisking
it in for another 5 minutes or until
glossy. Stir in the rose water.

Line a baking sheet with a silicone
baking mat or baking parchment. Pipe
or scoop the meringue mixture onto the
baking sheet and create a slight dip
in the middle. Bake for 2 hours.

Let it cool on the baking sheet, then
carefully remove the baking mat or
baking parchment and transfer the
meringue to a platter.

Put the passion fruit juice in a medium
saucepan and reduce to a syrup over
medium-high heat. Let it cool. Then cut
open the passion fruit and scoop the
pulp out into the syrup.

Assemble the pavlova by scooping a
billowing layer of Coconut Whipped
Cream or whipped Soy Whip into the dip
in the middle of the meringue, then
pouring the syrup on top, letting it
drip over the sides.

Pâte de Fruits

Serves 4

This recipe lends itself to all kinds of flavors and alcohols. There are some unusual ingredients (pectin, glucose syrup, and citric acid), but it's worth buying them for future use, as they don't cost much, don't go off, and you can use them for many other recipes. Try flavors like passion fruit, quince, or as I've done here, blackberry. And try adding Champagne for a "kir royale"-flavored pâte de fruits.

4 tsp [12 g] yellow pectin (available online at www.lepicerie.com or www.amazon.com)

2¾ cups [550 g] superfine sugar

18 oz [500 g] blackberry or other flavored purée, such as passion fruit (buy it or make your own, see right)

3 Tbsp [70 g] glucose syrup

Scant ½ tsp [3 g] citric acid (available at www.bulkapothecary.com or in Asian food stores)

½ cup [100 g] granulated sugar, for dusting

Equipment:

Digital thermometer

Plastic container, 4 by 8 in [10 by 20 cm], lined with enough plastic wrap to hang over the sides

Mix the pectin and ¼ cup [50 g] of the superfine sugar together in a small bowl or cup. Have this ready next to your stovetop.

Heat the purée in a medium, heavy-bottomed saucepan to medium-hot, then whisk in the pectin and sugar mixture. Bring to a boil, then pour in the remaining 2½ cups [500 g] superfine sugar and the glucose syrup. Measuring on a thermometer, bring the mixture to 225°F [107°C] and continue to boil at that temperature for a few minutes until it appears to be slightly thicker than jam.

Take off the heat and add the citric acid, then pour into the plastic container to set. Chill in the fridge for 1 hour or until set, then unmold and cut into diamonds or cubes.

Pour the granulated sugar into a shallow dish and turn the diamonds or cubes in it to coat liberally.

To make blackberry purée:

Blend 18 oz [500 g] blackberries (frozen if not in season) with ½ cup [100 g] superfine sugar and 3 Tbsp lemon juice. Then push through a strainer to remove all the seeds. Put this in a medium, heavy-bottomed saucepan and warm until the sugar has dissolved and the fruit has thickened slightly. Remove from the heat, allow to cool, and then set aside until ready to use. This will keep in the freezer for 3 months.

Blueberry Soup

Serves 4

18 oz [500 g]
  fresh or frozen
  blueberries

Scant 1½ cups
  [350 ml] water

Scant to heaping
  ½ cup [60
  to 75 g]
  superfine sugar,
  depending on
  how sweet you
  like it

Juice of ½ lemon

1 glass of vegan
  sweet white
  dessert wine
  or Madeira
  (optional)

2 Tbsp cornstarch

This is a dish I discovered on a trip to Sweden, although hot fruit soup is also a thing in Eastern Europe. As well as blueberries, blackberries, raspberries, and strawberries, the Swedes can forage for cloudberries, bilberries, lingonberries, and seabuckthorn berries. Berries are considered a superfood; full of antioxidants and vitamin C, plus anti-aging properties. The Swedes, in the summer, serve refreshing and healthy fruit soups with bilberries or rose hips, but I love blueberries.

Slowly simmer the blueberries, water, sugar, and lemon juice together. Once the blueberries have started to disintegrate, continue to simmer, adding the sweet wine if you wish. Then strain the soup, pushing it through a strainer with a wooden spoon.

Mix the cornstarch to a paste with a few tablespoons of water. Add this to the warm, strained blueberry soup. You could then put it through a blender to make it even smoother. Serve warm or cold.

Orange Flower Water, Cardamom, & Coconut Rice Pudding

Serves 2 to 3

Coconut oil,
  for oiling

Scant ½ cup
  [80 g] short
  grain rice

½ cup [100 g]
  superfine sugar

1⅔ cups [400 ml]
  coconut milk

1¼ cups [300 ml]
  water

2 Tbsp orange
  flower water

5 green cardamom
  pods

A highly perfumed version of a classic pudding.

Preheat the oven to 325°F [160°C].

Use a little coconut oil to lightly oil a shallow ovenproof dish, about 8 in [20 cm] square. Combine the rice, sugar, and coconut milk in a large bowl. Add the water (you can put it in the can of coconut milk, rinsing out the last bits of coconut).

Stir, then transfer to the prepared dish and add the orange flower water and cardamom pods. Bake for 90 minutes, stirring 3 or 4 times during cooking, until the rice is tender.

Put the dish under a hot broiler for 10 minutes to get a brown skin on top. Serve hot or cold.

Three Cherry Jelly Roll Trifle

Serves 4 to 6

For the jelly roll:

2 cups [260 g] self-rising flour

2 tsp baking powder

1 tsp sea salt

2 ripe bananas, peeled

Juice of 1 lemon

1⅛ cups [220 g] superfine sugar, plus 2 Tbsp for sprinkling

1 tsp vanilla paste

Scant ½ cup [100 ml] olive oil

½ cup [120 ml] water

For the filling:

7 oz [200 g] vegan margarine

Heaping 1 cup [150 g] powdered sugar

5¼ oz [150 g] canned or frozen sour cherries, drained and pitted

For the jelly:

1⅔ cups [400 ml] cherry juice

1 cup [200 g] superfine sugar

⅔ cup [100 g] fresh cherries, pitted

Scant 1 cup [200 ml] sloe gin, Malibu, or cherry brandy

2 level tsp agar-agar powder

Yes, you can make vegan trifle. The jelly is set with agar-agar, so do pay attention to how many grams of agar powder you put in, otherwise it sets as solid as a rock, which isn't what you want in a jelly. There is also a split between those who think the jelly should be on top and others who believe the jelly should be the bottom layer. One could write a PhD thesis on this kind of thing.

Sour cherries aren't easy to get hold of, but you can buy them canned, in a jar, or frozen from Middle Eastern suppliers and online.

As you assemble, make sure the coils of jelly roll can be seen through the sides of the glass bowl. This should be a billowing "froufrou" dessert in red and white.

You will need a jelly roll pan, or a baking sheet plus nonstick baking parchment.

Obviously the jelly roll and the jelly can also be served as separate desserts.

Preheat the oven to 400°F [200°C]. Line a jelly roll pan or baking sheet with good-quality baking parchment.

Combine the flour, baking powder, and salt in a bowl and set aside. Then in another bowl or in your stand mixer, beat together the bananas, lemon juice, and sugar, then beat in the vanilla paste and olive oil. The mixture should be fluffy.

Gradually fold the flour mixture and the water into the creamed banana mixture, then pour into the lined pan and spread it flat with an offset spatula. Bake in the oven for 10 to 12 minutes, or until the top is springy to the touch.

Remove it from the oven and clear a space on your worktop to do the next very important stage of making a jelly roll. Sprinkle the 2 Tbsp superfine sugar over the sponge while it is still hot. Put

cont'd...

Three Cherry Swiss Roll Trifle (cont'd...)

To assemble:

1 cup [150 g] morello or black cherries, pitted

1 cup [250 ml] vegan whipped cream (from an aerosol can is best)

⅓ cup [50 g] fresh cherries, left whole with stems

Powdered sugar, for dusting

another sheet of baking parchment over the sponge, and grabbing each side of the still-hot pan with your oven gloves, flip it over quickly. Remove the pan and leave the sponge to cool for 5 minutes, still covered on both sides with baking parchment.

For the filling, in a bowl or stand mixer, beat the vegan margarine with the powdered sugar, then add the sour cherries. Combine until you have a fluffy pink cream.

Remove the top sheet of baking parchment from the fairly cool sponge. Spread the filling, using a rubber spatula or an offset spatula, over the sponge. Then, starting from the short end, and using the bottom layer of parchment to aid you, carefully roll up the sponge and cream layer into a roulade shape. Imagine you are rolling sushi! Still in its parchment, wrap the jelly roll tightly in plastic wrap and chill in the fridge until ready to use.

To make the jelly, put all the ingredients in a medium saucepan and bring to a boil. Simmer for 5 minutes, then take off the heat and let it cool. It's important not to use too much agar-agar powder or it will set too hard and have an unpleasant mouthfeel; better to have slightly less than more, and every brand has its own strength, so it's hard to see until it sets whether it has jelled or not.

To assemble, remove the jelly roll from the fridge and take off the plastic wrap. Using a sharp knife, slice the roll into ⅝-in [1.5-cm] slices. Line the bottom and sides of a glass dish with the slices. Then fill the bottom with a layer of morello or black cherries. Pour in the cooled jelly to cover the cake and cherries, leaving space on top for the cream, and put it in the fridge to set (you may not need all the jelly, depending on the size of your trifle dish).

Once the jelly has set, either squirt or pipe thick vegan cream onto the jelly, dotting it around the edge and the center. Add the ⅓ cup [50 g] fresh cherries, stems sticking up. Dust with powdered sugar and serve.

Slow-Roasted Strawberries with Crunchy Bars & Raspberry Powder

Serves 6 to 8

This is a kind of alternative Eton Mess (a dessert consisting of a rough mixture of whipped cream, pieces of meringue, and fruit, typically strawberries) with honeycomb rather than meringue. For this you will need a digital thermometer, which I recommend all cooks should buy anyway. You can get one for around $20. That's unless you know your stuff when it comes to sugar and can tell by the water method—dropping a little of the boiling sugar into a glass of water and seeing if it solidifies.

14 oz [400 g] strawberries

½ cup [100 g] sugar

Storebought vegan whipped cream or homemade Thick Soy Cream (page 30)

2 Tbsp freeze-dried raspberry powder (available from some supermarkets and online)

For the honeycomb:

4 Tbsp golden syrup or light corn syrup

1 cup [200 g] superfine sugar

1 Tbsp baking soda

Preheat the oven to 325°F [160°C].

Pick the leaves off the strawberries, leaving the stalks. Line a sheet pan with a silicone baking mat or a sheet of baking parchment. Spread the strawberries out, sprinkle over the sugar and roast for 30 minutes. Let cool and reserve the syrup.

Line a baking pan, around 8 in [20 cm] square, with baking parchment or foil.

Put the syrup and sugar in a medium saucepan over high heat, and stir occasionally until it reaches 300°F [150°C] (the hard crack stage). Then, working quickly, add the baking soda and pour it all into the prepared baking pan. Leave to cool, then cut the honeycomb into 2-in [5-cm] pieces and remove from the pan.

Assemble the dessert just before serving, on a plate or in a glass for each person. Add layers of strawberries and syrup, honeycomb, and whipped vegan cream or Thick Soy Cream, in that order. Sprinkle the freeze-dried raspberry powder on top and serve.

Roast Persimmons with Coconut Tapioca Pudding

Serves 6 to 8

Tapioca is a love or hate food, probably because of childhood memories or school lunches. I, for one, like the pearl-like texture of tapioca pudding. Tapioca is a starch. It isn't a form of pasta, like semolina, but from the cassava root. It has virtually no nutritional value whatsoever!

For the tapioca:

1⅔ cups [400 ml] boiling water

2 cups [300 g] small pearl tapioca

1⅔ cups [400 ml] coconut milk

½ cup [100 g] superfine sugar

Pinch of sea salt

For the roast persimmons:

½ cup [100 g] coconut palm sugar, plus extra shavings to serve (optional)

Scant ½ cup [100 ml] boiling water

4 persimmons

3 star anise

Thumb of ginger, peeled and finely grated

1 cinnamon stick

Preheat the oven to 400°F [200°C].

Pour the boiling water into a saucepan and add the pearl tapioca. Cook for 5 minutes over medium heat, stirring constantly, then add the coconut milk, superfine sugar, and salt. Cook over low heat for another 10 minutes. Keep stirring, as it sticks easily. When the tapioca pearls are translucent, they are cooked.

For the persimmons, put the coconut palm sugar and boiling water in a saucepan and stir over medium-low heat until the sugar melts, to make a simple 1:1 syrup (1 part sugar to 1 part water).

Cut the persimmons in half or into slices and place in a baking pan. Add the star anise, ginger, and cinnamon stick to the pan. Pour over the syrup and roast in the hot oven for 10 to 15 minutes, or until the edges are starting to caramelize.

With the tapioca still warm (it can also be served cold), portion it out into glasses, cups, or small bowls, adding half a persimmon or a few slices on top of the tapioca. Add shavings of palm sugar to the top, if you like.

Summer Pudding with Preserved Ginger, Lime, & Coconut Cream

Serves 6 to 8

Scant 2 lb [850 g]
   berries (blackberries,
   raspberries, strawberries
   cut in half, blueberries),
   washed and stemmed as
   appropriate

1 cup [200 g] superfine sugar

2 to 3 balls of preserved
   ginger in syrup, thinly
   sliced

1 Tbsp coconut oil or
   vegan spread

8 to 10 slices of day-old
   thin, white, crustless
   bread

To garnish:

Mint leaves

Cornflowers or borage flowers

To serve:

Coconut Whipped Cream
   (see page 30)

Finely grated zest of 1 lime

Equipment:

1-qt [1-L] pudding basin,
   or Mason Cash steam bowl

This recipe doesn't need any change to become vegan. It's a British summer classic and easy to make. You'll need a 1-qt [1-L] pudding basin or steam bowl (a ceramic Mason Cash one is worth looking for.) Make sure the bread is stale, as it will hold the pudding together better. Only unmold just before serving.

Put all the fruit, sugar, and preserved ginger in a large, heavy-bottomed saucepan and simmer over medium-low heat for 5 to 10 minutes until all the sugar has dissolved. Then remove from the heat and set aside. Once cool, drain off some of the juice into a shallow dish.

Grease the pudding basin with the coconut oil or vegan spread. Dip the slices of bread into the juice and use to line the sides and base of the pudding basin. If you run out of juice, drain off some more from the fruit.

Spoon the fruit into the bread-lined basin, then add more slices of bread to cover the top, so that all the fruit is encased in fruit-soaked bread. Then place a saucer (which fits inside the rim) over the bread and a heavy can of food or weight on top of the saucer. Chill in the fridge for at least a couple of hours.

To serve, dip the bowl briefly into hot water, then flip it over onto a serving plate and lift off the basin. Garnish with mint leaves and cornflowers or borage flowers. Serve with Coconut Whipped Cream mixed with the lime zest.

Selection Box of Raw Chocolates

Makes approximately 12 chocolates

7 Tbsp [100 g] cacao butter, chopped

3 to 4 Tbsp cacao powder

½ tsp finely ground sea salt

4 Tbsp agave nectar or brown rice syrup, or ½ cup [100 g] superfine sugar

Flavoring options:

Finely grated lemon or orange zest

Lavender sugar

Ras el hanout spice mix (decorate with a rose petal)

Chopped nuts: hazelnuts, walnuts, pecans, almonds

Decoration options:

Candied violets

Rose petals

Silver or gold leaf

Glitter or other cake decorations

Equipment:

Chocolate mold or flexible ice-cube mold

I suggest you buy a chocolate mold for these or use a flexible, bendy ice-cube mold. Once the ingredients are melted down, the mixture is liquid and therefore you need to pour it into a mold, then chill it until set.

Do not confuse cocoa and cacao! Cacao is raw, unroasted cocoa beans, which are the dried and fermented beans you find in the cacao fruit, from which all chocolate comes. The rest of the fruit tastes rather like custard apple (cherimoya). Cocoa is the roasted version of the ground-up beans which releases the oils and the "butter." (Photo on page 164.)

Put the cacao butter in a heatproof bowl and set the bowl over a pan of boiling water so that the bottom of the bowl is not touching the water. Melt, then add the cacao powder, salt, and agave nectar, syrup, or sugar.

If not using flavorings, pour into your clean, dry mold, put straight into the fridge or freezer and leave to cool for a couple of hours. Then pop the chocolates out from the mold.

If using flavorings, decant the melted mixture into bowls and add the flavorings, taking care that the mixture doesn't start to cool. Then pour into the mold.

If using decorations, either pop them into the bottom of the mold or dab them onto the finished chocolate at the end with a touch of melted chocolate.

Variation: If you add a little nut milk and sweetener, you will end up with a thick chocolate paste that will set less hard. Once cooled, you can roll this into small balls and then roll in cocoa powder to make truffles.

Fleur de Sel Chocolate Peanut Butter Cups with Popping Candy

Makes 6 large cups

You need a silicone cupcake pan for this recipe. This way you can "paint" the chocolate inside, then peel off the insides.

- 7 oz [200 g] vegan dark chocolate, broken into pieces
- 2 Tbsp vegetable shortening, such as Crisco
- 1 scant cup [200 g] smooth peanut butter
- 2½ cups [300 g] sifted powdered sugar
- 3 Tbsp virgin coconut oil
- 1 tsp pure vanilla extract
- 1 tsp fleur de sel or other good quality sea salt
- ½ cup [75 g] popping candy

Equipment:

Silicone cupcake pan

Put the chocolate and shortening in a bowl and melt in the microwave for 30 seconds. Take it out, give it a stir and then microwave for another 30 seconds. If it needs a little more time, stick it in for another 30 seconds. Do not do it for longer bursts or it will ruin (or "seize") the chocolate. Set aside some of the mixture, to cover the tops.

Then with a clean, dry pastry brush, paint the insides of a silicone cupcake pan with the melted chocolate. Paint it quite thickly, leaving it to dry, then paint a second layer. (You want it fairly thick so that you can release it from the silicone without it breaking.) Put it in the fridge to set.

Combine the peanut butter, powdered sugar, coconut oil, vanilla, and salt in a medium saucepan. Heat gently over low heat until melted, then whip together with a whisk or rubber spatula until smooth. You don't want it too hot.

Remove the chocolate-lined silicone pan from the fridge and scoop 1 Tbsp of the peanut butter mixture into each hole to reach just below the top. Then smooth it over. Leave to chill in the fridge while you prepare the next stage.

Heat the reserved chocolate in a bowl set over a pan of simmering water, or give it 15 seconds in the microwave. Then add the popping candy. Paint or spoon the mixture carefully over the top of your peanut butter cups. Chill once more in the fridge for about 10 to 15 minutes or until set.

Remove the pan from the fridge and, using your thumbnail, release each peanut butter cup round the sides from the silicone. Gently pull away the silicone and push up from the bottom to remove each cup.

Index

A

achiote 14
agedashi tofu in broth 106
ajo blanco 86
alcohol 6
alfalfa seeds, sprouting 24—5
almonds: ajo blanco 86
apples: apple salad 147
artichoke, potato, spinach, & tofu
  b'stilla 162
avocados: black & green cheesecake 166
    guacamole 51

B

baba ghanoush 53
baechu kimchi 23
bananas: cashew, banana, &
  apricot smoothie 62
bean slider 107
beets: beet pelmeni 128
    mosaic of beets & radishes 94
    smoked basil & beet tofu 140
black & green cheesecake 166
black bean chili 72—3
black cabbage chips 45
Black Cat pancakes 66
black-eyed peas: ital stew 144
    Jamaican rice & peas 151
blueberries: blueberry sauce 74
    blueberry soup 178
bread: cornbread 150
    mini bunny chows 112
    sourdough bread crumbs 16
    summer pudding 184
    things on toast 42
    truffled sourdough bruschetta 69
broccoli: freekeh with purple sprouting
  broccoli 118
brownies, vegan 174
bruschetta, truffled sourdough 69
b'stilla 162
bunny chows, mini 112
butters, nut 31—2

C

cabbage: pickled purple cabbage 138—9
    Russian stuffed cabbage rose 156
    sauerkraut 22—3
cakes 45, 174
callaloo: ital stew 144
caramel: coconut salted caramel 170
    honeycomb 182
carrots: carrot, pepper, & lentil
  tagine 117
    roasted carrot dip 52
cashew nuts: black & green cheesecake 166

cashew, banana, & apricot smoothie 62
    nut roast 154—5
    smoky chipotle cashew cheese 33
"ceviche", lettuce cups with 98
cheesecake, black & green 166
"cheez", basic nut 32
chermoula 16
cherries: three cherry jelly
  roll trifle 179—81
chestnut purée: chocolate, orange,
  chestnut, & tofu mousse 168
chia seed, rose, & raspberry falooda 172
chickpeas: hummus 46—7
    roasted chickpeas 55
    sweet potato falafel slider 107
chiles 18—19
    black bean chilli 72—3
    chipotle tomato sauce 138—9
chimichurri 15
chocolate 13, 22
    chocolate, orange, chestnut,
      & tofu mousse 168
    chocolate Sichuan pepper
      fettuccine 125
    chocolate smoky tofu mole in tacos 142
    fleur de sel chocolate peanut
      butter cups 187
    Mexican chocolate shake 63
    selection box of raw chocolates 186
    vegan brownies 174
chowder, popcorn 88
chayote, ginger 146
citrus fruit 13—14
coconut 18
    coconut & cilantro dip 102
    coconut, lime, & chile sambal 82
coconut milk: coconut salted caramel 170
    coconut smoothie 62
    coconut tapioca pudding 183
    coconut whipped cream 30
    orange flower water, cardamom, &
      coconut rice pudding 178
    sweet potato & coconut
      South Seas soup 82
color wheel of food 38—9
corn cobs: popcorn chowder 88
cornbread 150
cosmetics & clothes 6
couscous, fluffy 116
cranberries: Russian stuffed cabbage
  rose 156
cream, nut 29—30
crumble, rhubarb 169
crumpets 64
cucumber: soy tzatziki dip 52
curry: mini bunny chows 112
custard 169

Acknowledgments

This book came about because of a vegan supper club collaboration between myself and Terry Hope Romero. I was talking about how successful it was to Ed Griffiths, head of publicity at Quadrille, and this is the result! So thank you to both Terry and Ed.

I'd like to thank Carolyn Stapleton of Black Cat (vegan) café, formerly the infamous anarchist vegan co-op Pogo café, in Clapton for her advice.

Thanks to my vegan testers:
Monica Shaw of Smarter Fitter, Gloria Nicol of The Laundry, Lucy Pearson, Josie Price, Lisa Roberjot, Michelle Eshkeri of Lavender Bakery, Linda Mazure, Diana McAllister, Carolyn Stapleton.

Thanks to my agent Michael Alcock.

Thanks to Catherine Phipps for her words of wisdom during the lonely process of writing a book.

Thanks to the brave and visionary team at Quadrille for commissioning this beauty of a book: Jane O'Shea, Helen Lewis, editor Céline Hughes, Simon Davis, designer Anita Mangan, food stylist Alice Hart (and her assistant), prop master David Herbert and photographer Jan Baldwin.

To my dad, John Rodgers, who has recently come to learn the benefits of a vegan diet

First published in 2015 by Quadrille Publishing Limited

Text © Kerstin Rodgers 2015
Photography © Jan Baldwin 2015

Quadrille is an imprint of Hardie Grant
www.hardiegrant.com.au

Quadrille Publishing Limited
Pentagon House
52—54 Southwark Street
London SE1 1UN
www.quadrille.co.uk
www.quadrille.com

ISBN 978 184949 6780

British Library Cataloguing-in-Publication Data. A catalogue record for this book is available from the British Library.

Publishing Director: Jane O'Shea
Creative Director: Helen Lewis
Art Director/Designer: Anita Mangan
Photographer: Jan Baldwin
Food Stylist: Alice Hart
Props Stylist: David Herbert
Production: Stephen Lang and Vincent Smith
Americanizer: Lee Faber

Printed and bound in China

www.cooked.com